SCULPTURE OF ANCIENT WEST MEXICO

Nayarit, Jalisco, Colima

The Proctor Stafford Collection

Michael Kan
Clement Meighan
H. B. Nicholson

Los Angeles County
Museum of Art
July 7-August 30, 1970

Printed in the United States of America
Library of Congress
Catalog Card Number 72-130462
S.B.N. 87587-040-6

COVER: Cargador with Five Pots,
Colima, see number 120;
FRONTISPIECE: "The King" (detail),
Jalisco, see number 86.

Contents

FOREWORD

What we know of the ancient artistic tradition of the far west of
Mexico, in that arc-like region along the Pacific that includes
the present-day states of Colima, Nayarit and Jalisco, has not
come from vast and dramatic temple complexes, or stone sculpture, or frescos and reliefs. They were not typical of the region.
Our knowledge of this unique West Mexican tradition has come
instead from a profusion of remarkable clay tomb figures and
related ceramic "burial furniture" that a people placed with their
dead nearly two thousand years ago.

These compelling hollow figures reflect totally human attributes. The pot carriers and "mourners," the embracing couples,
the "warriors" and "ball players"—even the dogs, the birds and
other animals—are in sharp contrast to the awesome and ritu-
alized deity figures of the later and better-known Mesoamerican
civilizations.

While the appealing 'humanity' of ancient West Mexican
clay sculpture has long been recognized, the acceptance of many
of these works as true *fine art* has been a slower matter.

In presenting this first public exhibition of the distinguished
Proctor Stafford Collection, seen only by specialists and scholars
until now, the Museum emphasizes its conviction that much
ancient sculpture from the far west of Mexico constitutes a high
and original form of art. While the works also serve as mute
spokesmen for early cultures, they cannot be regarded in a solely
historical, sociological, or anthropological context. Some are
consummate examples of sophisticated artistry. Indeed, a few
are masterworks in their own right. The time has come to regard
them for their aesthetic worth.

A superb collection such as this bespeaks much of its assem-
bler. Mr. Stafford began his collection during a long residence in
Mexico. He gathered the nucleus in an exciting time, with the
help of other knowing eyes, including those of Diego Rivera,
who chose to see in these pieces the origins of so much of the
humanity and vitality that is the glorious Mexican heritage.

Collecting, for Proctor Stafford, is a highly personal considera-
tion. Persistent and discriminating at all times, his only criteria
have been authenticity, quality, and concentration in a particular area. Like many true collectors he applies a somewhat anthropomorphic view, and the process of refinement that goes on in
all significant collections has often found joy coupled with
anguish, for one always has favorites that go by the wayside. The
Museum is grateful indeed for this opportunity to share with its
Members and the public the results of his many years of pain-
staking and fruitful connoisseurship.

Perhaps one of the most dramatic recent revelations to be
given currency by this exhibition is confirmation by colleagues
at the University of California that many West Mexican tomb
objects are of a much earlier date than had hitherto been con-
jectured. Until 1965 it was accepted by many that the substance
of this exhibition derived from a Mexican 'medieval age', with
some observers suggesting that the period extended into the
Spanish Conquest. A majority took the view that these appealing
works, possibly because of an assumption that sophistication is

late in the human scheme, dated variously from the 8th to the 10th centuries. But radiocarbon dating of objects and human bones by the University of California at Los Angeles in 1965, 1966, and more recently has proven that some actually derive from the second century before Christ! Thus we find, in West Mexico, a far longer and remarkably consistent artistic tradition than earlier research had thought possible, from about 200 B.C. through A.D. 500.

The preparation of the exhibition and of this catalog has been a loving labor for all who have had a hand. Certainly the Museum has leaned heavily on Guest Curator Michael Kan, Associate Curator of Primitive Art and New World Cultures at The Brooklyn Museum. Professors Clement Meighan and H. B. Nicholson, Department of Anthropology at the University of California, Los Angeles, who are pioneers in the area of West Mexican archaeology, have been of immeasurable help. Our gratitude extends also to Isabel Kelly, José Luis Franco, and Otto Schöndube for their review of the catalog index.

Within the Museum staff, Exhibitions Coordinator Jeanne Doyle was 'worried through' all stages of the exhibition and catalog. Head Photographer Edward Cornachio has applied his usual exacting standards in documenting an exceptionally challenging collection. Registrar Gloria Cortella has had prime responsibility for temporary custody of the objects. The catalog was designed by Ed Kysar, who also produced its line drawings and map. The exhibition itself was mounted by Associate Curator of Design and Allied Arts, William Ezelle Jones, with the assistance of Head Preparator James Allen and his able staff. Mr. Stafford has himself been ever available and generous with his advice and time. Appreciation also goes to Ann Koepfli for her constant assistance in the preparation of the catalog.

The Museum also warmly acknowledges a grant from the Ethnic Arts Council of Los Angeles, permitting the inclusion of color plates in the exhibition catalog. Dr. George C. Kennedy, former Chairman of the Council, was instrumental in securing the original C-14 dates from San Sebastián.

In recent years the Los Angeles County Museum of Art has been privileged to present several major exhibitions of art from pre-Hispanic Central and South America. *The Art of the Ancient Maya* was offered by the Museum in 1959. *Masterworks of Mexican Art,* seen by an astonishing 800,000 visitors, was made possible with the extensive cooperation of the government of the United States of Mexico in 1963. And many visitors will recall *Mastercraftsmen of Ancient Peru,* organized by the Solomon R. Guggenheim Museum, and presented in Los Angeles with the cooperation of the government of Peru in 1969.

The present exhibition continues the tradition of our concern.

Rexford Stead
Deputy Director

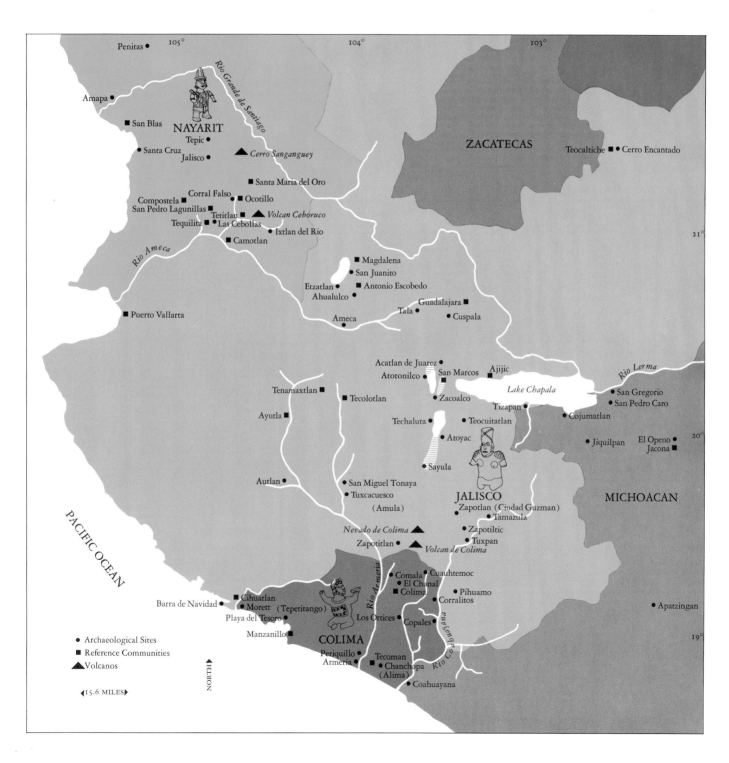

Penitas • 105°

Amapa •

■ San Blas

NAYARIT

Tepic •

• Santa Cruz
Jalisco •

▲ Cerro Sanganguey

■ Santa Maria del Oro

Corral Falso •
Compostela ■ • Ocotillo
San Pedro Lagunillas ■
Tetitlan ■ ▲ Volcan Ceboruco
Tequilita • • Las Cebollas
• Ixtlan del Rio
■ Camotlan

Rio Grande de Santiago

104°

ZACATECAS

103°

Teocaltiche ■ • Cerro Encantado

21°

Rio Ameca

• Puerto Vallarta

• Magdalena
• San Juanito
Etzatlan • • Antonio Escobedo
Ahualulco •
Ameca

Tala • Guadalajara ■
• Cuspala

Rio Lerma

Acatlan de Juarez •
Atotonilco • San Marcos • Ajijic ■
• Zacoalco
Lake Chapala

Tenamaxtlan ■
• Tecolotlan
Ayutla ■

Techaluta • • Teocuitatlan
• Atoyac

Tizapan •
• Cojumatlan

• San Gregorio
• San Pedro Caro

• Jiquilpan

El Openo •
Jacona ■

20°

• Sayula

Autlan •

• San Miguel Tonaya
• Tuxcacuesco
(Amula)

JALISCO
Zapotlan (Ciudad Guzman) •
• Tamazula

MICHOACAN

PACIFIC OCEAN

Nevado de Colima ▲
Zapotitlan • ▲ Volcan de Colima

• Zapotiltic
• Tuxpan

Comala • • Cuauhtemoc
• El Chanal
Barra de Navidad
■ Cihuatlan
• Morett (Tepetitango)
Playa del Tesoro •
Manzanillo ■

■ Colima
• Pihuamo
Corralitos •

Los Ortices • Copales •

COLIMA

Periquillo •
Armeria •

• Apatzingan

Rio Armeria

Rio Coahuayana

Tecoman •
• Chanchopa
(Alima)
• Coahuayana

19°

• Archaeological Sites
■ Reference Communities
▲ Volcanos

NORTH

◀15.6 MILES▶

THE
PRE-COLUMBIAN ART
OF
WESTERN MEXICO
Nayarit, Jalisco, Colima

Michael Kan

Both in terms of aesthetic quality and a feeling of spontaneity in handling the ceramic medium, Western Mexico must be ranked with Jomon Japan and Neolithic Anatolia, for its outstanding early figure sculpture tradition. The great hollow figures, which form the major portion of the Proctor Stafford Collection, are found in the Mexican states of Nayarit, Jalisco, and Colima, areas which in turn, have given their names to the principal West Mexican styles.

Art historical interest in the ceramic art of ancient Western Mexico may be said to begin at the turn of the century with the writings of Carl Lumholtz, inasmuch as he devoted several chapters in his well-known work *Unknown Mexico* to a qualitative and aesthetic discussion of the objects which he collected, mostly from the region of Ixtlán, Nayarit. Although he mistakenly considered these early figure types to be the art of the Tarascans, who inhabited Western Mexico at the time of conquest, he nevertheless was able to make some intelligent stylistic distinctions on the basis of his small sample of sculptures.[1]

Between the era of Lumholtz and the 1930's there appears to be very little archaeological or art historical interest in Western Mexico. During this period scholars were attracted primarily to the study of those Mesoamerican cultures which had produced writing systems, monumental architecture, and large-scale stone sculpture—all cultural traits associated with the Old World.

This bias towards high cultural achievements appears to have been shared by art historians and collectors as well as archaeologists. Until quite recently the art of Western Mexico has been referred to as "folk art."[2] Even the pioneer Mexican art historian Miguel Covarrubias displayed a certain bias when he stressed the "anecdotal"[3] and "absurd"[4] qualities of West Mexican art.

In the 1930's and 1940's important early collectors of pre-Columbian Mesoamerican art such as Robert Woods Bliss tended to concentrate their collecting on pre-Classic and Classic Period stone sculpture. Powerful Aztec stone carvings and small, precious Olmec and Mayan jades were the order of the day. If ceramic sculpture was acquired at all, it was probably from the Classic Gulf Coast, and even today, the Bliss Collection contains only one or two examples of West Mexican sculpture.

The notable exception to the typical collector of thirty and forty years ago was Diego Rivera, whose unique foresight and vision in collecting pre-Columbian art were shared by Proctor Stafford when he began to collect. Rivera's concentration in the West Mexican field enabled him to bring together the first group of Nayarit, Jalisco, and Colima figures which one could have called a collection in depth. Rivera's own prestige as one of Mexico's foremost painters undoubtedly contributed to the recognition of West Mexican art at the art museum level. In any event, his many years of collecting culminated in the publication of his collection in 1941 in a book, unfortunately with an unreliable text[5], and later, in the first exhibition dealing exclusively with the art of Western Mexico. This was the memorable show based primarily on the Rivera collection at the Palacio de Bellas Artes, Mexico City which opened in 1946. Emphasis was on the sculpture of Nayarit, Jalisco, and Colima, but objects from Michoacán were also shown. The catalogue, containing over one hundred and fifty illustrations and articles by Salvador Toscano, Paul Kirchoff, and Rubín de la Borbolla, was an important contribution to the archaeological and art historical knowledge of Western Mexico. Toscano's article was one of the first to differentiate between Tarascan art and the styles associated with Nayarit and Colima. In his scheme, however, Jalisco and Colima were under one heading. Rubín de la Borbolla's article dealt with the Tarascans and the state of Michoacán.

Kirchhoff's work is perhaps the most important from the art historical point of view, for it was an attempt to study the ancient people of Western Mexico through analysis of the costumes and ornaments found on their figure sculpture. On this basis, he established three categories which he believed to represent distinct social and ethnic groups.[6] First, "The Nudes," an ethnic group without dress, major in Nayarit, but of inferior status in Colima; second, "The Ones with Polychrome Garments" a group that showed a greater variety of costumes and occupied the southern portion of Nayarit; and third, "The Loincloth Group," whose members were clothed in a variety of breechclouts and were considerably more advanced than the others. Kirchhoff was no doubt influenced in his assessment of this last category by his belief that "The Loincloth Group" may have been essentially the same group that ruled a powerful kingdom in Colima at the time of Spanish contact.

Although Kirchhoff's work is of limited use today, in terms of our present knowledge of the West Mexican area, it was the first serious attempt to arrive at a typological classification of figure sculpture employing stylistic analysis. Unfortunately, the majority of the traits he used to characterize his types cut across clearly delineated stylistic differences, and totally disregarded possible chronological subdivisions.

If the *Bellas Artes* exhibition of 1946 was responsible for the recognition of Western Mexico as an aesthetic and art historical entity, it also served to focus the attention of Mexican and North American archaeologists on this area. By the end of the year a *Mesa Redonda* or "Round Table Conference" was held to gather together the scattered archaeological work which had been done in Western Mexico. Although the meetings were attended by a few art historians such as Miguel Covarrubias, very little information appeared on the ancient West Mexican sculpture complex. However, the well-known archaeologist Isabel Kelly, in a paper entitled "Ceramic Provinces of Northwestern Mexico" introduced the concept of an individual Jalisco style which she dubbed "Ameca" after the Ameca Valley in Jalisco State.[7]

Miguel Covarrubias' classic work of 1957, *The Indian Art of Mexico and Central America* ordered the art cultures of Western Mexico in much the same form as we know them today. The term "Tarascan" was used only to designate the culture which

flourished after the tenth century in the area of Lakes Pátzcuaro, Zirahuén, Cuitzeo, and Yuriria, and not as the earlier catch-all term used to cover the ceramic sculpture of the Nayarit, Jalisco, Colima area. His definition of this art culture area is still one of the best, and is worth quoting here: *A compact and fascinating group of cultures with an important art based upon the free-hand modeling of small and large hollow clay figures and effigy-vessels, made in the Pre-Classic tradition, as offerings to bury with the dead. They are found in tombs in the area now occupied by three Mexican states, Nayarit, Jalisco, and Colima, which has been for many years an inexhaustible mine of archaeological specimens.*[8]

The intuitive eye of Covarrubias, which had aided so much in solving the "Olmec problem," (enabling him to date Olmec art in the pre-Classic Period on stylistic grounds) also permitted him to see the stylistic kinship between the West Mexican figure complex and the pre-Classic figure traditions of the Mesoamerican heartland. Although he was aware of Isabel Kelly's dating of the figures found at Los Ortices, Colima and Ameca-Zacoalco, Jalisco in the early Classic Period,[9] he appears to have been completely justified in his visual-stylistic point of view. The early figures of Western Mexico seem totally devoid of classic traits from areas like Teotihuacán, and are much closer in feeling to pre-Classic Tlatilco or Zacatenco-Ticoman.[10]

George Kubler (1962), whose general volume *The Art and Architecture of Ancient America* devoted considerable space to a discussion of West Mexican art, chose to disregard Covarrubias' classification of "Jalisco" as one of the three major stylistic subdivisions. Instead, Jalisco (Ameca Valley) figures were classified as "a recognizable group within the Colima style.[11]

One of the most interesting aspects of Kubler's 1962 chapter on Western Mexico was his attempt to form a typological classification and seriation of the figure complex. Although severely limited by the meager and confused nature of his data, Kubler was able to form a seriation based on comparative technical details, differences in texture, and range of figural poses. A developmental sequence spanning several centuries was then suggested for the regions of Colima; Ixtlán del Río, Nayarit; and Ameca, Jalisco. The earliest style was characterized primarily by a coffee-bean eye type; the intermediate period, by a slit eye; and the latest and most developed, by eyes with modelled eyeballs.[12]

As opposed to Classical archaeology, which has traditionally belonged to science and the humanities, New World archaeology has always been linked to anthropology. However, as a historical tradition, New World archaeologists such as Herbert Spinden, have in fact contributed greatly to pre-Columbian art history. Thus, it is not surprising that two of the most recent and significant art historical contributions to the knowledge of West Mexican style should come from works which were primarily non-art historical, the 1966 doctoral dissertations of Stanley Long and Peter Furst.

Stanley Long's thesis entitled *Archaeology of the Municipio of Etzatlán Jalisco,* contains the most complete stylistic analysis of Nayarit ("San Sebastián Red") and Jalisco figures based on a group of seventeen found in tomb Number 1 at San Sebastián in the Magdalena Basin. A comparative study of ninety-one figure attributes ranging from technique and form to ornamentation and objects carried in the hand, divided the figures into two major groups.[13] Long considered the "classic" Nayarit (San Sebastián Red) figure type to be the earliest, both in terms of style and the consistently large and numerous areas of manganese oxide on its surfaces.[14] A second, and more developed Jalisco style of figure was called "El Arenal Brown." This type appeared to incorporate mold-made elements, and because of its more elaborate attributes was thought to have been produced by a people who were more socially stratified.[15] The "classic" Jalisco figures (Isabel Kelly's "Ameca Grey"), found in other tombs of the area, were classified as an intermediate style since they seemed to share the characteristics of the two major groups found in tomb Number 1 at San Sebastián.[16]

In the tradition of anthropologists like Herbert Spinden, Peter Furst represents par excellence a scholar who unites the humanistic and anthropological approach to the art of Western Mexico. His work at the important site of Las Cebollas near Tequilita in southern Nayarit provided significant information concerning the dating of the Nayarit shaft tomb complex. It also enabled him to establish a provenience and perform a complete study of an important Nayarit figure substyle known to the dealers and collectors of Mexico City as "Chinesco."[17] These so-called "Chinesco" figures were sufficiently limited in their geographical distribution and were of such outstanding aesthetic quality, that Furst suggested that they might represent the productions of a single "school," a concept which is certainly more art historical than the view commonly taken by anthropologists of the "anonymous tribal artist."[18] Furst's distrust of simplistic interpretations has also led him to some highly imaginative theories regarding the iconography of the West Mexican figures. Turning away from the "obvious" interpretation of a given figure pose (i.e., male figure holding club indicates "warrior"), Furst, borrowing from his ethnographic knowledge of the Huichol, was able to make an excellent case for the importance of shamanism in the iconography of the figure complex.[19]

Western Mexico as a Style Area

West Mexican art, for the purposes of this catalogue of the Proctor Stafford Collection, will be confined to the ceramic figure sculpture found mainly in tombs in the area of the present Mexican states of Nayarit, Jalisco, and Colima. Each one of these states in turn has given its name to a major figure type on the basis of certain stylistic traits. However, it should always be emphasized that these subdivisions are based on style rather than geography. It is now clear, for example, from Stanley Long's work in the Magdalena Basin, Jalisco, that typical Nayarit figures (San Sebastián Red) can occur in the same tombs (in the geographic area of Jalisco) with figures of the characteristic Jalisco type.

In marked contrast to the rest of Mesoamerica and particularly to the Guerrero style area in the south, the Nayarit-Jalisco-Colima style area is almost devoid of large scale lithic art, and only a few small carved stone figures and objects such as mace heads are found in areas like Colima. Besides the important unifying cultural features such as the great shaft tombs (found nowhere else in Mexico), West Mexican cultures appear to have focused their creativity on the manufacture of the larger hollow and smaller solid tomb figures. These clay sculptures share a dynamic and spontaneous force, a remarkable ability to capture the essence of a gesture in sculpture, and above all, a unique plastic force in the handling of the ceramic medium. Use of the ceramic techniques of incising and painting in both positive and negative slip colors is original and outstanding even in the total art production of Mesoamerica, one of the great pottery producing areas of the world.

Although the shortcomings of the three generally accepted catch-all terms for Western Mexico—Nayarit, Jalisco, and Colima—are known to all students of the area, they will continue in common use until these areas are better known to archaeology, and typological classifications which are meaningful both in time and space can be made. The glaring problem with typological seriations in the past has been the fact that they were based on the ordering of data taken from objects without provenience. Since it would have been impossible to check this data against material for which a reliable chronology had been established, the temporal and spatial significance of the typological classifications would have remained a total mystery and rendered the classification almost useless. In the art of the European west, this would have been the equivalent of recognizing that a painting was stylistically Venetian but not knowing whether it was painted in the fifteenth or eighteenth century.

The following three sections of this essay are devoted to a stylistic analysis of West Mexican styles and will concentrate on the stylistic relationships and distinctions between categories of figures. Although this study will be based almost entirely on the extremely large and varied sample of figures represented by the Proctor Stafford Collection, it cannot pretend to be anything approaching a comprehensive and systematic typological analysis. For this, one will have to await a work which is presently being undertaken by Hasso von Winning.

Nayarit

The figures of Nayarit show the largest range and variation of any West Mexican figure style. They are characterized by their generally expressionistic, active forms, with emphasis on both positive and negative painting. Arms usually are treated as long thin ropes of clay, with little attention given to naturalistic anatomical detail. In the Nayarit figures, relative to other styles, great attention is given to the rendition of hair which is indicated through a texture created by many fine incised lines. Characteristic articles of costume for the male figures include a distinctive shirt reaching to the sex organs, which are frequently covered with a "scoop loincloth" (see Nos. 13 and 16), and a small mantle tied with a cord over one shoulder (see No. 19, figure on left). Female figures wore a longer loincloth which somewhat resembled a sarong. Both sexes wore elaborate multiple-ring earrings which look like inverted fans, nose ornaments, and a characteristic type of facial mutilation which consisted of long vertical slits in the cheeks near the mouth (Nos. 64, 65). In certain instances figures are shown "threaded" together on a horizontal stick (Nos. 20, 23) through these cheek mutilations in a ritual unique to Nayarit. This ritual, like other ceremonies involving self-mutilation in Mesoamerica, may have been of a penitential nature.

The Nayarit figure style may be tentatively broken down into three major sub-categories. First, there is the Ixtlán del Río type of southern Nayarit (Nos. 12-24, 26-38, 43, 44); second, the "Chinesco" type (Nos. 1-11) also of southern Nayarit; and the San Sebastián Red type which comes from the states of both Nayarit and Jalisco (Nos. 25, 54-69).

Figures of the "classic" Nayarit type of Ixtlán were among the first West Mexican ceramic figures to be recognized, for Lumholtz illustrated at least seventeen in Plates I-IV of the second volume of *Unknown Mexico* in 1902. Although Lumholtz in effect realized that there were stylistic differences in the group of figures which he collected,[20] no scholar has ever really made the distinction between the more naturalistic (Nos. 12 and 15) and the more abstract (Nos. 13, 14, 16-24, 26-38, 43-44) varieties of Ixtlán figures. If we compare the Stafford male figure of the naturalistic type (No. 12) with a male figure of the abstract type (No. 16), the difference is immediately apparent. Although the costumes are similar in type (note for instance the same conical headdresses), the former has more naturalistic body proportions and more realistic modelling of arms and toes. The latter has the typical "elephantine" legs which are also characteristic of the San Sebastián Red category, with toes only barely indicated in a rough manner. Elaborate designs in white and yellow adorn the short-sleeved shirt and are again typical of this abstract variety of Ixtlán figure.

The abstract category of Ixtlán material has frequently been termed "absurd" and "brutal,"[21] yet it is one of the most spontaneous and expressive traditions of clay sculpture ever produced by man. If figures of this type covered with sores (Nos. 24 and 43) are grotesque, they are also highly expressive and poignant. The variety of activities are virtually endless: couples eating and preparing food (No. 18), men playing with their pets (No. 36), a full-scale West Mexican version of the ballgame complete with spectators (No. 34), and finally the famous house scenes (Nos. 27, 30 and 38). The latter are particularly intriguing and are unmatched for the wonderful tales which they depict. One in particular, "The House by Moon-

light" (No. 30) is truly lyric—a group of ravens and parrots is shown as though it had just alighted on the house eaves. Another striking group scene probably shows the West Mexican version of the volador ceremony (No. 35), and is a tiny masterpiece of asymmetry and sculptural balance. The clay has been handled so deftly that the figures give the impression of arrested movement.

"Chinescos" represent a type known to early collectors of southern Nayarit material but were not well-known until the early sixties. Although distinctive qualities are observable in the "Chinesco" group, these distinctions are often subtle and hard to pinpoint. It is possible, however, to distinguish four sub-categories within this broad Nayarit subdivision. First, the "classic Chinesco" (No. 1) which is characterized by a high degree of naturalism, majesty of pose, and subtly modelled eyes and face planes, and extremely high polish; second, a type with heart-shaped face, small coffee-bean eyes, and extensive painting on face and body in black (No. 2); third, a sub-category with squared head and slit eyes (Nos. 3, 4, 7, 11); and fourth, the so-called "Martian" type which is generally treated in a deep red slip either unpainted or overpainted with a cream slip (No. 6). Several other examples are illustrated in Furst's dissertation.[22]

"Classic Chinesco" figures (No. 1) possess the unusual quality of being monumental and exquisite at the same time. They differ from the average West Mexican figure and are more akin to the high culture art of Mesoamerica inasmuch as their calm subtle exterior suggests inner emotions rather than showing them overtly. The poses are generally static, and female figures usually have their legs tucked under them or thrust to the side. Arms and hands retain the rope-like Nayarit characteristic and are not as naturalistically rendered as the eyes and other facial features. Perhaps the most extraordinary naturalistic feature of this type is the way in which the half (or archaic) smile is suggested with such haunting realism. Peter Furst felt that these monumental (some have been reported to be almost three feet high) "Chinesco" figures which were found at Las Cebollas may have been created by a single "school."[23] Indeed, the famous seated "sister" to the Stafford "Chinesco" female (No. 1) in the National Museum of Anthropology in Mexico City[24] is so similar that there is every chance that both are by the hand of the same master.

Figures in the third and fourth sub-categories of "Chinescos" are by far the most common. The representations, mostly of females, are shown with legs outstretched to the sides and arms either to the sides or resting on the abdomen (Nos. 3, 4, 7). Other poses represented by Nos. 2 and 11, the former seated with arms crossed over upraised knees, and the latter, kneeling with one knee supporting crossed arms, are somewhat rarer types.

The "Martian Chinesco" figures have faces which are almost heart-shaped, shoulders which tend to be angular with great emphasis on the well-known shoulder knobs, and legs and feet which often stick straight out in front of the figure. The coloring of these pieces ranges from burnished red orange to a much darker red. Animals are rare in the "Chinesco" sub-category, and besides the toad (No. 10), there is a charming dog (No. 9) which is hard to classify because its highly burnished surface is so covered with burial patina.

One of the most familiar sub-categories of Nayarit is the San Sebastián Red type, a type that may be more at home in the geographical area of Jalisco than in Nayarit. These figures were studied in great detail by Stanley Long whose analysis of their stylistic features still represents the most complete study.[25] The San Sebastián Red substyle (Nos. 25, 54-69, 73) is one of the most familiar of all types within the Nayarit style, and most West Mexican sculpture collections are rich in these figures with their dynamic expressive poses. "Classic" figures of this substyle (25, 54-56, 60-65) are characterized by deep red paste color clouded with black burial patina (black manganese deposits), positive and negative painting primarily in black and cream slip, no navels indicated, only occasional nose rings (unlike Ixtlán), elaborate incised indications of hair, and eyes and mouth indicated by punched wide slits. There are two variants which can be noted in the Proctor Stafford Collection: first, what Long calls the Ojos Variant,[26] which is intermediate between San Sebastián Red and "classic" Jalisco (Ameca Grey), and is distinguished by its eye type with applique ridges and naturalistic mouth and an indication of teeth; and second, the "pointed ears" type (Nos. 68 and 73), which again, seems to have Jalisco characteristics.

San Sebastián Red figures bring to mind, almost more than any other West Mexican sculpture, the highly expressive qualities of clay modelling. Some, like the small reclining male figure (No. 60) convey a sense of arrested movement; others, like the three emaciated "mourners" (No. 62) are more static in pose but just as expressionistic in the way in which tensions are built into the composition. The Warrior and Mate (Nos. 64 and 65) are perhaps the most "classic" examples of the substyle, the female with her body covered with both positive and negative painting, and the male sporting his familiar bicorn helmet and body "armor," creating a most interesting abstract composition.

Until recently the so-called "Zacatecas" figures have been tentatively classified as Nayarit (see pages 50, 51). These little-known figures (Nos. 39-42) with their strangely modelled heads, pierced eyes, mouth, and disc earrings, hair tied in the form of horns (on the male figures), and positive and negative body painting do not readily relate to other types. The extensive negative and positive paint covering most of the body does conform to the Nayarit style. The typical figure poses are also in keeping with certain Nayarit substyles. The seated females (Nos. 39 and 42) have their hands to the sides and legs extended out in front. The males (Nos. 39, 40) are seated with legs bent and raised up. Long rope-like arms (another Nayarit feature) are crossed over the raised legs, sometimes holding a drum between the legs. A convention which one sees in the "Zacatecas" figures which is most extraordinarily similar to Nayarit is the manner in which the raised leg, bent at the knee, is treated as a simple upright support at right angles to the extended leg (compare Nos. 40 and 62).

Jalisco

The Jalisco style can be subdivided into three basic substyles: first, the "classic" Jalisco which is also known by Isabel Kelly's term Ameca Grey (Nos. 74, 76, 78, 81-85, 95, 99); second, the substyle named El Arenal Brown by Stanley Long (Nos. 86 and 98); and third, the substyle of the Municipio of Antonio Escobedo (No. 87). To these one can tentatively add a little known type which can be called the "Elephantine" type because of its general appearance of heaviness, especially in the legs (Nos. 96, 97).

Ameca Grey or "classic" Jalisco figures are either cream or red slipped or a combination of both (as in No. 76). One of the most distinctive features is the tremendously elongated occipitally-deformed heads which are either decorated with applique ornament which criss-crosses the head, or in the case of male figures, are frequently shown wearing a crested helmet (see large figure in No. 83). Female figures not uncommonly have large breasts tattooed with spiral designs, and nipples modelled in applique (No. 81). Other distinctive features of the head include the characteristic large staring eyes rimmed with thick fillets, an aquiline, almost hatchet-shaped nose, and a large open mouth in which the teeth are clearly defined.

"Classic" Jalisco figures are often in interesting yet static poses. An exception would be the magnificent crouching warrior (No. 74) holding a striped shield in one hand and a mace or dagger in the other. His body is beautifully balanced and poised in a position which is most unusual for Jalisco figures. A second figure, outstanding for its scale and high surface polish, is the "Wrestler" (No. 85) which is also much less frontal and rigid than the average Jalisco figure of the Ameca Grey type. Like its Olmec counterpart, the famed "Corona Wrestler," its balanced but flowing asymmetrical composition imparts a feeling of great physical power and suppleness of limb. Without suggesting cultural or stylistic ties, the highly burnished light grey-cream surface of this figure, spotted in fire-clouded areas with darker grey and reddish "blushes," is highly reminiscent of the well-known hollow "baby face" Olmec figures from Tlatilco and Las Bocas.

Several poses, or should they be called "themes," reoccur with some regularity. One can refer particularly to such representations as the Rite (No. 83), "The Pot Marker" (No. 99), Joined Couple (No. 84), and the "thinkers" (such as "Pensive Woman," (No. 95), which are almost always women with long "sarongs" which drape gracefully over the raised knee. Solid figurines in the "classic" Jalisco style (e.g., No. 94) possess a more spontaneous quality than the large hollow ones, but do not begin to rival the solid figurine traditions of Nayarit (Ixtlán) or Colima in the elaborateness of group activity scenes.

Stanley Long felt that the culture that had produced the El Arenal Brown substyles was more advanced than any of the other peoples he studied in this area, and that their society was highly stratified.[27] When one studies the great thirty-seven inch warrior figure (No. 86) one can only imagine that this impressive character must have been a king,[28] as he is named in this collection. The other El Arenal Brown figure in the Stafford Collection (No. 98), though smaller, seems also to be filled with a latent energy and power. The figures of this substyle are almost always slipped red with details such as eyeballs painted in white. A lighter rust slip paint was also used to color details of costume. El Arenal potters must have developed great control of their firing methods, since the coarse textured brown paste, though only fired to low temperatures, must have been difficult to handle in an enormous figure such as The King.

A type of seated nude female figure with her hands upraised and legs extending out in front of her (No. 87), seems to combine a number of Jalisco and Nayarit features. The extreme elongation of head and long hatchet-shaped nose, and large breasts with applique nipples are features which point to Jalisco, while the general pose, treatment of the eyes and mouth, and fan-shaped multiple earrings seem to suggest the Nayarit style. These figures are said to come from the region of San Juanito, municipio of Antonio Escobedo (e.g., Parres Arias 1962).

Another little-known type is even harder to place (Nos. 96, 97, 100, 105). They have been grouped together on the basis of their color which can best be described as a burnished brown-grey. They have been dubbed the "Elephantine" sub-category since two of them (Nos. 96, 97) have the gigantic legs which we associate with Nayarit. The long rope-like arms may be thought of as another Nayarit characteristic, yet somehow the face of the figure carrying the pot on its shoulder (No. 96) has a head which suggests Jalisco proportions. With his head tilted back and a ball balanced on the end of his nose, his hands raised in an airy arc over his head, the Performer (No. 97) is certainly an expressive masterpiece. The balancing of the extremely heavy lower portion of the body against the airy upper portion provides a truly dynamic form.

A Warrior and Mate (No. 89) can be immediately recognized as a perfect San Sebastián Red-Ameca Grey hybrid. The bicorn helmet worn by the male and the large elephantine foot shared by both figures, is derived from the Nayarit style, while the facial features, general body proportions, and white slipped surface painted in red, are typically Jalisco.

Colima

Early Colima is probably the most homogeneous of West Mexican styles, for its famous hollow figures are unified by the familiar light orange to deep red burnished slip with spots of black patina scattered over the surface. On occasion, the black areas are so numerous as to make black the dominant color.

Black is also frequently achieved through reduction firing.

Colima ceramic art can conveniently be divided into four subcategories: first, the "classic" types ranging from anthropomorphic and zoomorphic representations, through effigy vessels to plain vessels; second, the solid figures; third, a hollow figure type with coffee-bean eyes (No. 125); and fourth, the probably Post-Classic types. In addition there are stone (No. 206) and shell (No. 203) objects which are found in tombs in association with "classic" Colima figures.

The "classic" Colima tradition provides a dazzling variety of human and animal figures along with an equally amazing selection of pots which range from elaborate effigy vessels (Nos. 119 and 121) to masterpieces of abstract form (No. 191).

Human figures, though shown in a wide range of poses, have a more mannered and less exuberant quality than the Nayarit figures of the San Sebastián type. Like opera singers on the stage, Colima figures such as the magnificent "Drinker" (No. 122) give the impression of being frozen in a mannered posture rather than being actually captured in movement. Here, too, is a prime example of the "classic" Colima use of certain selected techniques which were used over and over by Colima potters. An orange-red slip was first applied over the whole figure, then details of costume such as the head-strap and mantle were overpainted in a darker red. The piece would then be burnished, often with a smooth stone on the unbaked surface (see burnishing stones, No. 53). The darker areas were then engraved with extremely fine lines after firing to provide an exquisite network of delicate lines (No. 124). No wonder Colima figures have always been prized for their great polish and elegance.

Another masterpiece, Jorobado (No. 134), the seated hunchback dwarf, is the essence of pent-up force of the type which we associate with Olmec sculpture. The rounded volumes of the powerful but shrunken body are perfect complements to the disproportionately large brooding head. No form of engraving or other decoration has been introduced to conflict with this monumental statement of pure form.

Figures (Nos. 109 and 116) represent an interesting and more elaborate variation of "classic" Colima types. These representations sport unusually elaborate costumes, have eyes which must have originally held shell inlay, and are generally more angular in their facial planes than the average Colima figure. This type may represent an important ritual personage of some sort —a priest or shaman.

Colima is particularly noted for its wide range of zoomorphic representations, the most famous of which are dogs (Nos. 147 B, 152-154, 156). They are thought by some scholars to represent the emissaries of the God of Death, Xólotl, who led the dead on their journey to the underworld.[29] Another indication of the iconographic importance of the dog within the funerary context, is the fact that it is the only animal shown in Colima art wearing a human mask (No. 154). Actual life-sized human masks in ceramic (Nos. 148 and 150) similar to the one worn by the masked dog, are known in Colima art. Amongst the other wide range of animals portrayed one finds the Gophers (No. 161), the Crab (No. 163), the Horned Toad (No. 164), the Double-headed Snake (No. 170), the Parrot (No. 175), the Owl (No. 177), and the Water Bird (No. 171).

In "classic" Colima ceramic art there is an almost unbelievable range of forms from outright representations of figures, objects, animals, fruits, and vegetables, to effigy vessels, where supporting elements are modified into representations, to pure pots with beautiful abstract forms. The Yawning Man (No. 149) is a good example of the first variety, in which the whole vessel has been cunningly worked into the form of a human head, with the open mouth serving as the orifice. The finely detailed skeumorphic ceramic replica of a hafted double-headed stone mace (No. 151) is a good example, since for all its naturalism and detail, one never loses sight of the fact that it is a container.

The second variety includes the well-known tripod vessels, often in the form of some fruit or vegetable (Nos. 127, 128 and 165 and 188 and 189) on which animal or human elements are added as legs or simply as modifications to the body of the vessel. In other examples (Nos. 178-182, 184) the body of the vessel itself is modelled or modified into the shape of a fruit or vegetable. In the third variety (e.g., No. 186) are simple, highly sophisticated ceramic vessel forms, some of which (Nos. 190 and 191) have pure dynamic outlines which would have done credit to a potter of Sung China.

Solid figures in the Colima tradition can be visually subdivided into three rough categories; first, the flat highly-burnished brown-buff figures with "athletic builds" and bowed legs (No. 144); second, the flat "cookie" unslipped and unburnished types (Nos. 132, 135, 140-143, 145, 146); and finally, the solid unburnished figures in more three dimensional poses (Nos. 136-139, 147). Because of the similarity of their highly burnished surfaces, one would place the first category with the large hollow Colima figures of "classic" type, and be tempted to place the second category of the unburnished "cookie" figures on an earlier time level with similar pre-Classic figurines from Michoacán.

The third category of solid Colima figures has a great many of the qualities which have been referred to in connection with the Nayarit San Sebastián Red sub-category. Figures such as the Acrobat (No. 137) and Quarrel (No. 136) represent the epitome of vivacious movement.

A single large hollow figure (No. 130) is clearly of a different type than the "classic" Colima red-ware figures. Seated on a four-legged stool its pose is closely related to two well-known Colima figures in the Diego Rivera Collection.[30] One of the latter is of the "Marcelled" type and holds a bowl in the extended right arm, as does a similar figure in the collection of the National Museum of Anthropology, Mexico.[31]

Colima art objects of the post-Classic Period are really beyond the scope of this study. A type of sculpture loosely referred to by collectors and dealers as the El Chanal style includes the "incensario" (No. 199), a strange grotesque sculpture decorated with black paint.

Conclusion

This exhibition of the Proctor Stafford Collection will provide as important an occasion in the history of West Mexican art studies as the historic Palacio de Bellas Artes show in Mexico City in the 1940's. For the first time in the United States, groups consisting of many select examples of figure art from Nayarit, Jalisco, and Colima will be brought into focus rather than being dispersed among the other art styles of Mesoamerica.

Unfortunately, the scope of the preceeding essay has not permitted a discussion of the fascinating iconography of the West Mexican figure complex. As archaeology progresses in this area of Western Mexico a body of reliable data should soon be added to our present knowledge to make the study of pre-Columbian West Mexican iconography a truly fascinating field open to anthropologists and art historians.

Hopefully, the stylistic studies included here, as cursory as they are, will in a small measure aid in the great task of typological classification which still lies ahead of us.

As a final note, let us remember that these magnificent clay sculptures are only a small part of the artistic output of this ancient people: gone is their music and oral literature, their sculpture in wood, and their textiles. Although we will never know the names of their "Michelangelos" or "Brancusis," we can be very conscious that we are looking at the work of masters.

Notes

1 Lumholtz, Carl, *Unknown Mexico*, Vol. II, New York, 1902, pp. 308-309.
2 Bushnell, G. H. S., *Ancient Art of the Americas*, London, 1965, p. 102.
3 Covarrubias, Miguel, *Indian Art of Mexico and Central America*, New York, 1957, p. 87.
4 *Ibid.*, p. 89.
5 Medioni, Gilbert and Pinto, Marie-Therese, *Art in Ancient Mexico*, New York, 1941. In this book the term "Tarascan" was still being used

for Nayarit, Jalisco, and Colima; and there is no specific section on the art of Western Mexico.
6 Toscano, S., Rubín de la Borbolla, and Kirchhoff, P., *Arte Precolombino del Occidente de México*, Dirección General de Educación Estética Pública, México, 1946, pp. 49-64.
7 Kelly, Isabel, "Ceramic Provinces of Northwestern Mexico" in *El Occidente de México*, Sociedad Mexicana de Antropología, Cuarta

Reunión de Mesa Redonda sobre Problemas Antropológicos de México y Centro América, México, 1948, pp. 55-71.
8 Covarrubias, Miguel, op. cit., p. 87.
9 *Ibid.*, pp. 88-89.
10 Mr. Stafford's taste for the sculpture of pre-Classic Tlatilco tends to reinforce its visual kinship with West Mexican material.
11 Kubler, George, *The Art and Architecture of Ancient America*, Baltimore, 1962, p. 109.

12 *Ibid.*, p. 108-110.

13 Long, Stanley V., *Archaeology of the Municipio of Etzatlan,* Jalisco, Ph.D. dissertation, UCLA, Los Angeles, 1966, pp. 22-23.

14 *Ibid.*, p. 24. Since the exact nature of Long's "manganese oxide patina" is not traceable to a single source (see Gifford, 1950: pp. 200-201), this evidence would appear to be inconclusive.

15 *Ibid.*, p. 104.

16 *Ibid.*, p. 24.

17 Furst, Peter, *Shaft-Tombs, Shell Trumpets and Shamanism: A Culture-Historical Approach to Problems in West Mexican Archaeology,* Ph.D. dissertation, UCLA, Los Angeles, 1966, p. 15.

18 *Ibid.*, p. 35.

19 Furst, Peter, "West Mexican Tomb Sculpture as Evidence for Shamanism in Pre-hispanic Mesoamerica," *Antropologica,* No. 15, December, Caracas, 1965, pp. 73-76.

20 Lumholtz, op. cit., pp. 308-309.

21 Covarrubias, *op. cit.*, p. 89.

22 Furst, *op. cit.,* Plates 53-75, see also Gifford, Edward, *Surface Archaeology of Ixtlan del Río, Nayarit,* University of California Publications in American Archaeology and Ethnology, Vol. 43, No. 2, 1950, Plate 5A.

23 Furst, *op. cit.*, p. 35.

24 For an illustration of this piece see Bernal, Ignacio, *Museo Nacional de Antropología de México,* Mexico, 1967, Plate 290.

25 Long, *op. cit.*, pp. 62-79.

26 *Ibid.*, pp. 35-36.

27 *Ibid.*, pp. 23-24.

28 *Ibid.*, p. 79. Long believed that helmeted warriors were not represented in El Arenal Brown. This warrior type because of his pose must be closely related as an iconographic type to the typical San Sebastián Red warrior type with the bicorn helmet.

29 Toscano, *op. cit.*, p. 24.

30 *Ibid.*, Plate 43.

31 Bernal, *op. cit.*, Plate 290.

Chronological Chart of West Mexican Archaeological Cultures

STATE	NAYARIT			JALISCO						COLIMA				
ARCH. PROVINCE	NORTH NAYARIT	SOUTH NAYARIT		AMECA	CHAPALA	AUTLAN-TUXCACUESCO		RIO BOLANOS	CIHUATLAN	COLIMA			REFERENCE CHRONOLOGY	
SITE	Amapa Peñitas	Ixtlan		Magdalena		Autlán	Tuxcacuesco	Totoate	Navidad	Morett	Tesoro		BASIN OF MEXICO	PERIODS
	Amapa			El Arenal							UCLA 1034 UCLA 148			
500		Early Ixtlán del Río						GX 610 GX 609		UCLA 187			Xolalpan (Teotihuacán III-IIIA)	
400	Gavilán			UCLA 593C UCLA 1032 UCLA 966							UCLA 797 UCLA 912 UCLA 910			Early Classic
300				Ameca									Tlamimilolpa (Teotihuacán IIA-III)	
200	Tamarindo UCLA 973	Tequilita Shaft-Tomb UCLA 1012					Tuxcacuesco			Ortices— Chanchopa Chanchopa Tomb UCLA 1066			Miccaotli (Teotihuacán II)	
100								Early Totoate			UCLA 911 UCLA 909 UCLA 790 UCLA 798		Tzacualli (Teotihuacán I-IA)	
A.D. B.C.		San Sebastián									Early Morett UCLA 795 UCLA 188		Chimalhuacán/Patlachique	
100													Cuicuilco/Tezoyuca	Late Pre-classic
200				UCLA 593A UCLA 593B									Ticoman III/Late Cuanalán	

Abbreviations and numbers, UCLA 593, etc., are numbers of radiocarbon samples that fall at the indicated time level and serve to date the associated named culture. Where these occur on the chart, direct dating of the remains by C-14 is indicated. Where they do not occur (e.g., Tuxcacuesco), it indicates that the age is estimated on the basis of stratigraphy and stylistic similarity with finds in other sites.

THE CERAMIC MORTUARY OFFERINGS OF PREHISTORIC WEST MEXICO
An Archaeological Perspective

Clement W. Meighan & H. B. Nicholson

Introduction

Our understanding of the extraordinary lost world of ancient West Mexico is only incipient. One of the greatest contributions which can be made to increased knowledge is the opening of important private collections to scholars. The present exhibition and catalog represent one major effort along this line. Although most of the Proctor Stafford Collection has never been published, it is an outstanding collection of West Mexican art and probably the finest Jalisco collection in the world. The first public presentation of this collection in a leading art museum is an especially appropriate occasion for a concise appraisal of our present knowledge of the ancient cultures of West Mexico whose patient, skilled craftsmen produced these remarkable creations in clay. At the same time, we hope to provide the reader a sufficient archaeological background to enable him to better understand and appreciate the specimens displayed and herein illustrated.

This exhibition also provides an excellent opportunity to combine archaeological and esthetic approaches to pre-Hispanic West Mexican art. Here, we discuss the Proctor Stafford Collection from the viewpoint of the archaeologist, leaving the discussion of artistic style to the accompanying analysis by Michael Kan.

The term "West Mexico" is a general one and can be variously defined. Here, we confine our discussion largely to the far western coastal states of Nayarit, Jalisco, and Colima. The region encompassed by these modern Mexican political jurisdictions has also been referred to as "Trans-Tarascan Michoacán West Mexico" (Taylor, Berger, Meighan, and Nicholson 1969). From this region, in terms of present knowledge, the pieces included in the present exhibition derive. Furthermore, as will be demonstrated below, much of the area of these three western states constitutes a distinct culture area in prehistoric times and can be conveniently treated as a unit.

Until recently, it was not possible for archaeologists to contribute much to studies of prehistoric West Mexican art because little formal archaeology had been pursued in the region. Only within the past decade or so have we been able to ascertain in some detail the age, provenience, and cultural context for most of the kinds of objects in the present exhibition. The Proctor Stafford Collection has much archaeological significance, in the light of recent investigations, for several reasons. First, it is a largely unified collection, the major portion of it from one well delimited region (Nayarit-Jalisco-Colima) and one principal time period (the centuries just before and after the start of the Christian era). It differs, therefore, from most large Mesoamerican collections which are more eclectic and diversified and contain objects from many quite distinct cultural and artistic traditions.

Second, the specialization of the Proctor Stafford Collection and its concentration on a group of closely interrelated styles provides it with both breadth and depth for this section of West

Mexico. The collection includes specimens of nearly all the recognized major varieties of West Mexican ceramic sculpture and often several examples of each type. It thus provides a generally representative sample of ancient far West Mexican art which no single excavation or group of excavations could hope to obtain.

Third, in selecting the pieces primarily on the basis of their aesthetic quality, Mr. Stafford has inevitably assembled an excellent cross-section of the best productions of these ancient artists. The exhibition is not to be taken as a display of ordinary manufactures, but rather of those objects on which the craftsmen lavished particular care and skill. Hence the collection includes the largest of the known tomb figures (No. 86) and many examples of those most carefully modeled and most elaborately decorated. Such a collection has real value to culture-historical studies in defining the upper limits of native ability in certain areas of human activity. It provides a basis for comparative study from which the finest productions of one group of people may be compared with their counterparts made at another time and place.

The archaeologist can contribute to a greater understanding and appreciation of the Proctor Stafford Collection in various ways. Above all, he can provide an approximately accurate chronology so that we know when the pieces were made. This is important historically, but until recently a correct temporal assignment was not possible. West Mexican artifacts were attributed to widely varying time periods spread over considerably more than a thousand years. We now know from radiocarbon dating that most of the types in the exhibition were made in the period from about 200 B.C. to A.D. 500 (see page 32).

Another major contribution of the archaeologist is the reconstruction of the cultural context within which the art objects were made and used. We can assess to some extent what the pieces were intended to represent, why they were made, and what they meant to the people who made them. The sculptured ceramic figures constitute an unintentional message from the past—from groups who left no written records of any kind—for these representations convey to us in artistic form many of their activities, manufactures, and customs. It is worth stressing, however, that the makers of these objects had no intention of transmitting information to us about themselves. What we can reconstruct concerning their vanished life styles depends upon archaeological interpretation.

The level of genuine civilization was reached in only two areas of the aboriginal New World: Andean South America and Mesoamerica. Within the latter area co-tradition, West Mexico is perhaps the most sharply differentiated sub-area, on the basis of both negative and positive criteria. Although displaying many of the most fundamental distinguishing marks of Mesoamerican civilization, West Mexico appears to have occupied a somewhat peripheral and less developed position vis-à-vis the Mesoamerican "heartland" to the east, particularly in the aesthetic, intellectual, and religious-ritual spheres. On the positive side, a unique mortuary complex with no close parallels elsewhere in

Mesoamerica flourished at an early period in one major sector of West Mexico: the shaft-chamber tomb with rich ceramic offerings.

Serious scholarly interest in pre-Hispanic West Mexico developed slowly in comparison with many other areas of Mesoamerica. Generally lacking the spectacular surface sites which gave impetus to archaeological investigation elsewhere, the more modest remains of the far West only gradually came under the systematic scrutiny of the professional scholar. Even today knowledge of the area is spotty and far from satisfactory. Ironically, principally beginning about 1927 with the completion of the West Coast railroad, out of this region has flowed an extraordinary quantity of superior ceramic figures and vessels. Probably for no other region of Mesoamerica, in fact, do we have available for study so many complete ceramic specimens. The great majority were removed from tombs and burials for sale by non-archaeologists and thus were extracted without any recorded observations of their context. The archaeologist is, therefore, confronted with a challenging problem. He has available a remarkably rich mass of information from the past in one major Mesoamerican sub-region. However, he faces formidable difficulties in utilizing it to reconstruct and explain that past since he knows virtually nothing about the precise proveniences and associations of these numerous pieces now scattered throughout hundreds of private and public collections. In short, he is simultaneously delighted and frustrated. This remarkable group of finds cannot be ignored, but it is extremely difficult to explain archaeologically.

The obvious solution to this archaeological dilemma would involve a comprehensive research program on three principal fronts: 1) field investigation, including systematic excavations, of as many of the cemetery areas and their associated occupation sites as possible; 2) the compilation of a master catalog of photographs of all known pieces, which would include all reliable provenience data; 3) more systematic analysis (technological, chronological, typological, ethnographic-interpretational, etc.) of presently available pieces, utilizing all relevant modern techniques and sources of information. In a broad sense, such a program—however uncoordinated and diffuse—has actually been under way ever since the first adequate publication, in the second half of the last century, of a West Mexican tomb piece

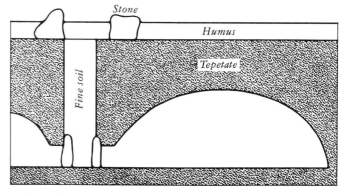

Colima Tomb (after Disselhoff 1932)

in a generally available publication. While our understanding of the ancient sculpture of West Mexico is only incipient, hundreds of pieces have now been illustrated, a few of the tombs—unfortunately nearly all at least partially looted—have been carefully investigated and recorded, general archaeological knowledge of the area has steadily advanced, and various analytic and interpretational studies are currently in progress.

Search and Research

Precisely when the first West Mexican mortuary pieces came to general attention is somewhat obscure. Certainly most of the early works on Mexican archaeology virtually ignored this peripheral area. Few pieces were adequately illustrated before the turn of the century. Then, in 1902, appeared *Unknown Mexico,* the classic account of the travels of a Norwegian explorer, Carl Lumholtz, in Northwest Mexico. Lumholtz (1902, Vol. II: *passim*) was the first to illustrate a sizable number of mortuary pieces he collected in Nayarit and Jalisco, with fairly specific proveniences. He also included the first generalized description of the type of shaft-chamber tomb common in the Ixtlán del Río area, a rifled example of which he visited in 1896. Already in his time widespread ransacking of tombs and burials was being vigorously pursued by the local populace. Although not the first to employ it, Lumholtz probably as much as anyone contributed to the propagation of the inaccurate and misleading label "Tarascan" for the large West Mexican mortuary ceramic figures—even though he was well aware they hailed from areas located west of any region known to have ever been occupied by Tarascan speakers.

A year later, in 1903, a British artist-archaeologist, Adela Breton, published an account of the discovery, in 1896, on the hacienda of Guadalupe (about 10 miles north of Etzatlán, Jalisco), of a burial in a large mound with rich mortuary offerings, including over 20 large ceramic figures. Drawings of three of these were included, plus some shell ornaments. Breton's brief article was important, for it pinpointed with unusual specificity the provenience and *in situ* associations, however general, of two of the most important (Long's San Sebastián Red and El Arenal Brown) Jalisco types of large anthropomorphic ceramic figures.

During the next few years steadily growing numbers of the mortuary pieces flowed out of the rich West Mexican earth. Increasingly, works on Mexican archaeology included them in their coverage, with Colima also receiving appropriate attention (a discussion of musical instruments in a Colima collection, which reached Berlin through a local consul, was published by Kunike as early as 1912). Local West Mexican historians often included some general notices on local antiquities, occasionally including illustrations. One of these (Galindo 1922, 1923-24, 1925) published the first general discussion of Colima archaeology which featured various illustrations of mortuary figures

—including the famous dogs—and the first generalized account of a Colima shaft-tomb. The growing appreciation of the aesthetic quality of the West Mexican mortuary pieces was signalized by the inclusion in one of the first comprehensive surveys of pre-Columbian art (Basler and Brummer 1928) of ten plates illustrating Nayarit, Jalisco, and Colima ceramic figures.

As indicated above, an influential event occurred in 1927, the completion of the West Coast Southern Pacific of Mexico railroad. This opened the whole area to a more intensive form of tourism which in turn stimulated the search for saleable archaeological pieces. A significant event in terms of professional archaeology occurred in 1930 with the entry of the University of California into the field, led by Sauer and Brand (1932). However, they concentrated initially on the far northwest (Sinaloa) and virtually no attention was devoted to the tombs and burials, and their contents, of the area farther south in the early stages of the UC program (subsequently carried on principally by Isabel Kelly).

Another important event took place in 1932 when a German archaeologist, Disselhoff, published the first detailed descriptions and diagrams of Colima tombs, based on field reconnaissance. His article also included a map indicating locations of cemetery sites and illustrations of ceramic figures with specific proveniences given (cf. Disselhoff 1936, 1960). He suggested a typology of four principal forms of tombs, two of which were of the shaft-chamber variety. Remarkably, to this day Disselhoff's articles remain the only detailed treatments of Colima tombs derived from actual field investigations.

The thirties saw the beginnings of the formation of some of the most important private collections, above all that of the leading Mexican painter, Diego Rivera. Pieces from these collections increasingly found their way into exhibitions of pre-Columbian art and into books and journals concerned with Mexican art and archaeology. In 1935, a local historian, Ramírez Flores, published a short article illustrating and describing various ceramic figures and vessels from the lake region of east central Jalisco (Zacoalco, Techaluta, Teocuitatlán, Atoyac). This contribution was of considerable importance because, like Breton's much earlier article, it pinpointed geographically a significant tradition distinct from those of Nayarit and Colima—although the author seems not to have recognized the specific mortuary origin of these pieces.

In 1938, a leading Mexican archaeologist, Eduardo Noguera, conducted investigations in El Opeño, a cemetery near Jacona (northwestern Michoacán), excavating and recording five shaft-chamber tombs with sloping entrance tunnels. Their contents were quite distinct from those of the shaft-chamber tombs of Nayarit-Jalisco-Colima, however, and their discoverer (Noguera 1942; 1965: 150-151) suggested ties with the Preclassic traditions of Central Mexico. Today, however, it is recognized that some connection with the vertical shaft-chamber tomb tradition farther west also seems likely, although the precise nature of this relationship awaits further investigation.

Beginning in 1939, as an extension of her work in Sinaloa, Isabel Kelly conducted reconnaissances and excavations through 1944 in various portions of the regions which yield the elaborate ceramic mortuary pieces (Kelly 1944, 1945, 1947a, 1947b, 1948, 1949). Her most significant discovery was a large restorable Teotihuacán style Thin Orange jar at the edge of a looted tomb at Chanchopa, near Tecomán, Colima. This became the principal support for equating the period of the West Mexican tombs and the ceramic pieces found therein with Classic Teotihuacán (111). In 1940 she also excavated several tombs at Los Ortices, near Colima, and one at Chanchopa, but these have not yet been published. She also advanced a scheme of four sequent phases for Colima: the Ortices (Classic) phase, i.e., the tomb period to which most of the pieces in the Proctor Stafford Collection relate; the Colima and Armería phases (both of them Early Postclassic); and the Periquillo phase (Late Postclassic). This phasing, only briefly summarized in various of her publications, for years served as the "standard" Colima archaeological sequence (she has since added a fifth phase, Comala, after Ortices). Kelly also surveyed and excavated during this period in the Autlán-Tuxcacuesco-Zapotitlán zone of Jalisco, just to the north of Colima, where, in the eastern portion of this zone, cemetery sites yielding mortuary pieces similar to those of Colima are not uncommon. Accordingly, she proposed that the earliest phase of the Tuxcacuesco region (designated by that term) was contemporaneous with the tomb period (Ortices) of Colima. Also in 1939 the most extensive publication of Colima mortuary pieces issued up to that time appeared (Cossío 1939, 1940), and two years later, in 1941 (Medioni and Pinto), a book entirely devoted to Diego Rivera's extensive collection was published, which included many of his West Mexican specimens. These two works made available to students a much greater corpus of the West Mexican mortuary pieces.

In 1946, Gifford (1950) conducted a surface survey (to provide a suitable archaeological context for a large collection of pieces from this region acquired by the University of California, Berkeley, in 1931) of the Ahuacatlán River drainage of southeastern Nayarit. He worked out a three-phase sequence, Early, Middle, and Late Ixtlán, the earliest of which corresponded to the period of the shaft-chamber tombs. He did not investigate the tombs themselves, however, other than to briefly inspect some emptied ones. Many figures of the "Ixtlán del Río type" were illustrated in this useful monograph, as well as various vessels and other objects associated with them. Gifford's descriptions of the ceramics of Early Ixtlán have not been superseded by any later work.

A major event of the same year was the first large exhibition devoted entirely to pre-Hispanic West Mexican art at the Palacio de Bellas Artes in Mexico City, sponsored by the Dirección General de Educación Estética. The majority of the pieces shown were from the Diego Rivera collection. The well-illustrated catalog (México Secretaría de Educación Pública, 1946) included three important essays by Toscano, Rubín de la Borbolla, and Kirchhoff. Toscano concentrated on an aesthetic appreciation, but he also dealt to some extent with ethnographic-iconographic aspects. Rubín de la Borbolla devoted his attention solely to Michoacán (east of the area which concerns us here). Kirchhoff concentrated on ethnographic interpretations. His article constituted the most serious discussion of this aspect hitherto published and is filled with valuable, perceptive observations. However, his basic breakdown of the anthropomorphic ceramic figures into three principal groups, "The Nudes," "Those with Polychrome Garments," and "Those with Loincloths," leaves much to be desired and is obviously somewhat distorting in its spatial-temporal connotations. Noteworthy is the failure anywhere in the volume to recognize the Jalisco traditions as being essentially distinct from those of Nayarit and Colima. Overall, however, this little volume represented the most important single contribution to the subject published up to that time.

Pointing up the greatly increased interest in West Mexico at this time was the Sociedad Mexicana de Antropología's Mesa Redonda devoted to this area, in the fall of that same year. The tombs and their offerings, however, received little attention in the conference report published in 1948. Only Kelly, in her important article on ceramic provinces of Northwest Mexico, devoted some discussion to this topic. She clearly recognized the distinctiveness of the Jalisco traditions, the most common of which she labeled "Ameca." She also hypothesized a more or less continuous arc of tomb cemetery sites, yielding the large figures as characteristic mortuary offerings, from Colima north through the Autlán-Tuxcacuesco, Sayula-Zacoalco, and Ameca-Etzatlán zones to the "Nayarit Hinterland."

Apparently in the forties, but not published until 1954, Corona Nuñez conducted some investigations of various cemetery sites in Nayarit, including some with shaft-chamber tombs. He described three principal types—bottle-shaped, "simple grave," and shaft and chamber—plotting their distribution on a map. His article included the first published diagrams of Nayarit shaft-chamber tombs: a double-chambered example in a cemetery at Corral Falso, near Ocotillo in the municipio of Santa María del Oro (including the layout of skeletons and mortuary offerings), and a single-chambered one at "Los Chiqueros, Ixtlán." He also suggested an intimate association between shaft-chamber tombs and agricultural terraces in the municipios of Santa María del Oro, San Pedro Lagunillas, and Compostela.

In 1955, the most spectacular tomb hitherto discovered, with three chambers and a 52 feet deep shaft, at El Arenal, near Etzatlán, Jalisco, was robbed. It was recorded and published, together with photographs of some objects supposedly found in it, by Corona Nuñez (1955). In 1962, at the suggestion of Nicholson and under the general sponsorship of UCLA, Stanley Long initiated an archaeological reconnaissance-excavation project in the Magdalena Basin where Etzatlán is located. A major purpose was to locate and excavate an undisturbed deep shaft-chamber tomb. Although Long, working two seasons (1962, 1963-64) with a proton magnetometer and a seismic hammer, failed in this objective, he did carefully investigate and record basic data on ten shaft-chamber tombs at five different sites in the basin. The more or less intact contents of one, San Sebastián Tomb 1, stripped in 1963 while Long was in the United States, were acquired by a U.S. museum and were intensively studied by Long (1966), who was able, working with an informant, to reconstruct with considerable accuracy the original layout of the mortuary offerings. Long's Etzatlán project was a landmark in West Mexican archaeology, and, because of its importance, is discussed in more detail below.

In 1965, Furst and Delgado salvage-excavated a partially looted shaft-chamber tomb with two chambers in an extensive cemetery at Las Cebollas, near Tequilita, southern Nayarit (Furst 1965, 1966; Delgado 1969). It contained various large figures of the type nicknamed by dealers "Chinesco," 125 conch shells, over 25 slate discs encrusted with pyrites, and various other mortuary offerings. Furst and Delgado during this period also surveyed a large number of sacked tomb cemetery sites in a region centered on San Pedro Lagunillas, Nayarit (Furst 1966, 1967).

The first application of radiocarbon dating to objects found in West Mexican shaft-chamber tombs also occurred in 1965, when three shells from San Sebastián Tomb 1 were dated at the UCLA Isotope Laboratory of the Institute of Geophysics and Planetary Physics (Furst 1965a, b; Long 1966; Long and Taylor 1966a, b; two determinations on human bones from this same tomb were later added). One of the conch shells from the Las Cebollas tomb was also dated at this time (Berger and Libby 1966: 475). Ranging between 200 B.C. and A.D. 330, these C14 tests established the chronology of the tomb period of West Mexican archaeology on a reasonably firm basis for the first time (see page 32). What some had suspected, but could not convincingly demonstrate, was now virtually certain: at least part of the period of the West Mexican tombs, and their characteristic mortuary offerings, was coeval with the Late Preclassic and Early Classic of Central Mexico.[1]

The most recent significant field investigations of various cemetery sites, including the excavation of four unlooted shaft-chamber tombs in two different locations, were undertaken by Delgado (1969). All four were of the type nicknamed by the looters "tumbas de la cueva" (cave tombs). Three were located near Cuspala, about 10 miles southwest of Guadalajara; the fourth was found at San Miguel Tonaya, approximately the same distance northeast of Tuxcacuesco. All, according to their discoverer, contained the figures known popularly as "muertos," small effigies of humans strapped to platforms (e.g., Nos. 101, 102). Various vessels were also found in the Cuspala tombs, while the Tonaya chamber also yielded a large hollow Colima style figure and a house model. Delgado also excavated a burial at Cerro Encantado, near Teocaltiche, northeastern Jalisco, which reportedly contained an assemblage of "Zacatecas" ceramic pieces, including a "horned figure" (cf. 39, 40, 41), three conch shells, and various other objects. Two radiocarbon dates, one on charcoal and the other on one of the shells, indicated an A.D.

second century date for this burial—which would make it contemporary with the shaft-chamber tombs farther west (Delgado 1969).

Finally, it should be noted that Kelly, the doyenne of West Mexican archaeology, is presently conducting surveys and excavations in Colima preparatory to publishing a comprehensive report on the prehistory of this rich area where she initiated serious professional work over thirty years ago.[2]

This brief historical résumé is not intended to be exhaustive, but hopefully includes some mention of most of the significant investigations and publications concerning the Nayarit-Jalisco-Colima zone particularly characterized by shaft-chamber tombs and burials containing elaborate ceramic offerings. It would be incomplete, however, to omit various publications of the past two or three decades not directly related to field investigations but which contain many valuable illustrations of mortuary figures and vessels (apart from numerous volumes devoted to pre-Hispanic Mesoamerican or general pre-Columbian art which almost invariably contain sections on West Mexico). Some of the most important of those devoted only to our area are: Medioni 1952, Collier 1959, Piña Chan 1959, Corona Nuñez 1960, Ramos Meza 1960, Instituto Jalisciense de Antropología e Historia 1964, Messmacher 1966, Alsberg 1968, and Schöndube 1968, 1969. Also worth special mention, because of the important information they provide concerning the provenances of various of the "Jalisco types," are a series of notes in *Eco* (journal of the Instituto Jalisciense de Antropología e Historia), 1960-1968, principally by Parres Arias, illustrating and briefly describing pieces in the Museo de Arqueología del Occidente de México, Guadalajara.

Environmental Background

As mentioned earlier, the geographical occurrence (see page 8) of pre-Hispanic West Mexican art of the characteristic forms found in this exhibition is largely restricted to the far western coastal states of Nayarit, Jalisco, and Colima. These states do not form a geographical unit. Apart from numerous "microenvironments," they consist primarily of two fundamental zones: a highland region with elevations averaging about 5000 feet and a relatively narrow coastal plain of tropical lowlands. The vegetation cover varies from savanna grasslands and deciduous tropical forests in the coastal regions, especially in Nayarit, to the vegetationally sparser parklands, upland grasslands, and pine-oak forests of the plateau basins and valleys. The highlands are largely volcanic in origin and form the western margin of the great Mesa Central, which comprises most of Central Mexico. From the high country there is often an abrupt drop to the coastal plain, particularly in the region of the southern Nayarit coast. After the great trough of the lower Banderas Valley (where Puerto Vallarta is located), to the south, in Jalisco, a rugged mountain barrier rises abruptly from the sea. As one moves south along the coast the narrow plain alternately widens and narrows, until, in Colima, it constitutes a broad coastal flatland, ending abruptly on the coast of Michoacán where a rugged massif again rises precipitously from the ocean.

Four major river systems drain the upland interior regions where the majority of the cemetery sites are located. In the north is the Río Grande de Santiago, the longest in Mexico, which issues from Lake Chapala in highland Jalisco-Michoacán and debouches on the coast north of San Blas, Nayarit. The southern Nayarit plateau and the highland area of central Jalisco, extending almost to Guadalajara, are drained by the Río Ameca system, southeast of which is a chain of north-south trending highland basins of interior drainage containing shallow lakes (Atotonilco, San Marcos, Zacoalco, Atoyac, Sayula, Zapotlán). West and southwest of this lake zone is the drainage system of the Río Armería, which bisects Colima. To the southeast, constituting in its lower reaches the Colima-Michoacán boundary, is the Río Coahuayana system, which drains eastern Colima, southern Jalisco, and southwest Michoacán. Three famous volcanic peaks dominate different sectors of the landscape: in the north, in southern Nayarit, Sangangüey and Ceboruco, and, in the south, the twin peaks of the Volcán and Nevado de Colima.

The great majority of the tomb sites are located in the upland zones. Recently, rather simple shaft-chamber tombs have been located close to the coast near Puerto Vallarta, Jalisco (Elerth Erickson, personal communication), but they do not appear to be common anywhere in the coastal plain. The West Mexican highlands constitute a zone of generally temperate climate with substantial rainfall in most areas and much fertile volcanic soil. The shallow lakes mentioned above are now mostly dry, partly through gradual dessication due to progressive climatic aridity and partly from intentional drainage in relatively recent times to reclaim agricultural land. Two to five thousand years ago the region was apparently somewhat better watered and must have supported an abundance of game (deer, peccary, rabbit, squirrel, opposum, etc.) and migratory waterfowl. It was undoubtedly a very favorable environment from the standpoint of its earliest settlers, both hunter-gatherers and cultivators. Although direct evidence for the beginnings of farming has not yet been found, it seems probable that early agriculture was practiced in this zone for several centuries before the beginning of the Christian era—and possibly much before. In any case, by the time of the birth of Christ, when the mortuary ceramic art was apparently flowering, considerable land must have been under cultivation, and the native game animals had become much less important as a food source than the products of farming.

Native Peoples of the Area at the Time of the Spanish Conquest

Most of the pieces in this exhibition probably came from shaft-chamber tombs—and the rest from burials. The shaft-chamber tomb cemetery sites are concentrated in an area which can best be described as a great arc extending north from Colima, through southern-central Jalisco, and, veering to the northwest, into south-central Nayarit. This extensive zone was well populated when the Spaniards arrived between 1522 and 1525. The first exploring parties in 1522-1523 just penetrated the eastern outposts of this area. They were commanded by Cristóbal de Olid, the lieutenant of Cortés sent to take over the Tarascan empire of Michoacán, and by his second-in-command, Juan Rodríguez de Villafuerte. The definitive conquest of Colima by the energetic Cortesian "constant captain," Gonzalo de Sandoval, occurred in 1523. An Amazon-hunting *entrada* more or less paralleling the arc on the west from Colima to the Ameca-Etzatlán zone, then squarely following it out to just south of the Río Grande de Santiago, was led in 1524-1525 by the *alcalde mayor* of the fledgling Spanish villa of Colima, Francisco Cortés (cousin of the great conqueror). Descriptions of the native cultures of the area written in connection with these expeditions of conquest are frustratingly meager, but various accounts contain spare but precious ethnographic information (summarized in Nicholson, ms.). Although many significant changes had obviously occurred between the time of the period of the shaft-chamber tombs and the Conquest, fundamental culture patterns were probably not too dissimilar, and there may have been many direct survivals from the earlier era. Consequently, in spite of the unsatisfactory state of our knowledge of the Contact peoples, what is known concerning their way of life can perhaps aid us to interpret the significance of the extraordinary objects they placed in their tombs centuries before the arrival of the conquistadores. A brief résumé of what is known about the Contact peoples of the "tomb arc," therefore, seems definitely in order.

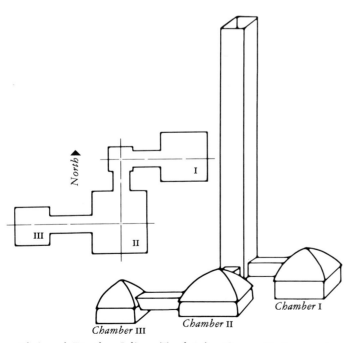

El Arenal, Etzatlan, Jalisco, Tomb (after Corona Nuñez 1955)

Beginning in the south, in Colima, knowledge of this area is very unsatisfactory. Colima at Contact was particularly thriving and populous (Sauer [1948:81] estimated a total population of 350,000 for "Greater Colima"), although reports in the uncritical and romantic later colonial chronicles of a great "kingdom" of Colima are obviously false. Rather, a cluster of essentially autonomous small provinces, the most important of which were called by the Spaniards, Alima, Tecomán, Colimotl (after the native ruler), Tepetitango, and Cihuatlán, constituted the overall "province of Colima" (see Sauer 1948), which may, in return for military assistance against those potent imperialists, the Tarascans, have paid a small token tribute to the Empire of the Triple Alliance (Tenochtitlán-Tetzcoco-Tlacopán). Apparently a rustic version of the Nahua, or Aztec, language served as a relatively recently imported *lingua franca* for this whole zone, which was otherwise characterized by a high degree of linguistic diversity.

The native culture, in general, appears to have represented a kind of reduced and simplified version of the typical high culture of western Mesoamerica, such as that of the Basin of Mexico ("Aztec culture"). A well established village way of life, based on productive agriculture, was flourishing. The capitals of the major provinces were large towns (perhaps up to 5,000-10,000). Their dependencies ranged from sizable villages to tiny *ranchitos*.

The usual Mesoamerican triumvirate of staple food plants, maize, beans, and squash, was supplemented by nutritious root crops such as the sweet potato, manioc (yuca), and the peanut. Also important were grain amaranth, chia, tomato, chile pepper, cacao (the beans used both as a source of chocolate and probably for currency, as elsewhere in Mesoamerica), and various fruits: pineapple, zapote, guava, ciruelas, etc. Cotton was grown in quantity, the bottle gourd was cultivated for containers, and tobacco (used in ritual and also believed to possess curative powers) was raised. Irrigation was commonly practiced where conditions permitted, and two annual crops were not uncommon in more favored locations. Turkeys, Muscovy ducks, and bees (honey production was important) were domesticated, as was the dog, one breed of which was probably castrated, fattened, and eaten.

Little specific information is available concerning native crafts, but it is clear that weaving was well developed, as was featherwork, ceramics, basketry, and probably woodworking. Architecture was apparently not very advanced. The typical dwelling was a small wattle-and-daub structure with a peaked thatched roof. The rulers undoubtedly possessed fairly large abodes but probably of the same general type as their subjects. Ceremonial structures were obviously important, but they are virtually undescribed. Certainly there was no elaborate stone and stucco ceremonial architecture of the type for which more highly developed regions of Mesoamerica are famous, nor was there stone sculpture of any great consequence, elsewhere one of the most brilliant arts of Mesoamerica.

The economic, sociopolitical, and religious-ritual aspects of the culture are poorly known. Markets and intra- and inter-community trade were important in adjoining regions, and they must have been in Colima as well. The rulers, particularly the paramount provincial chiefs, were undoubtedly supported by tribute, but details are lacking. Although it is unlikely that the social structure here was as complex as in the nuclear areas to the East, a certain amount of stratification must have characterized the society. Chieftainship certainly was well developed, and it is likely that some kind of native aristocracy played a significant leadership role. Unless Colima was completely atypical, religion and ritual must also have been of great importance. One late colonial source from an immediately adjoining area reports the cult of the basic Mesoamerican mother goddess of fertility and an opposing and contrasting fire god whose abode was believed to be in the Volcán de Colima. Human sacrifice was prevalent in nearby areas and was very likely important here, too. Militarism in general must have been well developed. The Tarascan-threat from the East had been successfully repelled, and at Tecomán the first invading Spanish party, under Juan Rodríguez de Villafuerte, was defeated. In West Mexico in general the basic weaponry consisted of the bow and arrow, the spearthrower (*atlatl*), sling, club, and mace. For protection, the shield of tough woven cane and padded cotton body armor were employed. The Colima warrior was undoubtedly similarly accoutered.

Directly north of Colima was a zone of rugged topography which extended to the upper Río Ameca valley and comprised the higher drainage of the Armería river. Various "provinces" were recognized by the Spaniards: Amula, Autlán-Milpa, Ayutla, Tenamaxtlán, Tecolotlán, etc. All seem to have been politically autonomous, although eastern Amula apparently for a time had been subject to Tarascan political control not long before the Conquest. Generally, with the exception of the Autlán-Milpa region, the culture of this zone appears to have been somewhat more rustic than that of Colima. Various dialects of a language called "Otomí" dominated the linguistic scene—although Nahua was certainly in some general use. Whether this "Otomí" was the same as the widespread, important language of that name of Central Mexico is uncertain. The Autlán-Milpa zone seems to have constituted an enclave of somewhat more advanced culture. Autlán was called a "city" by the earliest Spaniards to reach it and was credited with 1200 houses, certainly a large community for West Mexico.

Northeast of Colima was an important "province" dominated by three large centers: Tamazula, Zapotlán, and Tuxpan. They were considered by the Spaniards to be characterized by a superior culture and were also reputed to be active mercantile centers. Important silver mines existed near Tamazula, which were the first significant sources of this metal exploited by the Spaniards in Mexico and also apparently served as the major source of silver for the Tarascan dynasts of Tzintzuntzan. The linguistic situation in this area was particularly complex, with each major capital bi-, tri-, or even quadrilingual, although Nahua was in general use. Tarascan was also spoken to some extent, for the area was politically controlled by Tzintzuntzan at Contact. A little more is known of the religion of this area. A mother goddess appears to have played a preeminent role, and certain cosmological notions displayed a close similarity to those typical of Central Mexico.

To the northwest, directly east of the northern portion of the "Otomi" zone previously described, in the lake district of east-central Jalisco, was a group of substantial native communities which became known in early colonial times as the "Avalos province," after the relative of Cortés, Alonso de Avalos, who held most of the pueblos of this zone in *encomienda* (in trust, to receive their tribute). Probably not an integrated political unit, the region was apparently composed of various more or less independent *cabeceras* which were linked—perhaps by military alliances—by their common determination to preserve their independence against the formidable military power of the Tarascan empire. As is typical for far West Mexico, linguistic variety characterized the area, but two languages appear to have been dominant, Coca ("Pinome") in the north and Sayulteca (from Sayula, one of the major towns) in the south. The former may have been a Uto-Aztecan tongue related to Cahita (Yaqui, Mayo, etc.), while the latter may have been closely related to Nahua, if not just a dialect of it. Ethnographically this zone is even more poorly known than those previously discussed. The general level of culture, however, appears to have been relatively high, comparing quite favorably with Colima and the Tuxpan-Tamazula-Zapotlán area.

Following out the arc just before it turns sharply to the northwest, the next zone consists of the upper Ameca valley, the Magdalena Basin (with another large shallow lake), and the rolling plateau country to the east extending as far as Guadalajara and beyond. Ameca, which gave its name to the river on whose banks it stood, was the southernmost outpost of the famous Cazcan, who seem to have spoken a language closely akin to Nahua and whose center of gravity was in northern Jalisco-southern Zacatecas. Their formidable uprising in 1541 ("Mixton War") was the first great nativistic movement in the history of the New World—and had to be crushed by a large Spanish army led by Viceroy Antonio de Mendoza himself. Etzatlán, on the south shore of the lake of that name, dominated the Magdalena Basin, which was both Nahua (Cazcan?) and "Otomi" (Tecuexe?) in speech. The first Spaniards reported a ceremonial center on an island in the lake with stone substructures for shrines similar to those in the Basin of Mexico, indicating a relatively high cultural level for the area.

To the east was a great cluster of Tecuexe (linguistic affiliation uncertain) and Coca towns, extending well past Guadalajara and the Río Grande de Santiago to the frontiers of the "Gran Chichimeca," the great arid steppes of the North, the haunt of the fierce hunting-gathering peoples. A high degree of local political autonomy seems to have prevailed in this exten-

sive area, where Nahua again was in widespread use. The general way of life appears to have been quite similar to that which prevailed in the Ameca-Etzatlán region and the Avalos province to the south. This area had also successfully resisted Tarascan imperialistic encroachment.

The northwest segment of the arc begins west of a rugged mountain knot along the Jalisco-Nayarit border, in the Ahuacatlán valley. Rounding to the north the great Ceboruco volcano, the plateau of Tepic is reached which drops off sharply to the lowland zone around San Blas. This region was characterized by a broad strip of substantial native communities, rimmed on the north by the deep canyon of the Santiago River and on the south and west by rugged country which comprised the northern edge of the Río Ameca valley and the mountainous escarpment overlooking the Pacific coastal plain. The area is perhaps the poorest known from the standpoint of ethnographic specifics.

The Ahuacatlán valley was well populated with Iztlan (modern Ixtlán del Río) and Ahuacatlán in the valley proper, and Camotlan and Tetitlan, south and north of the valley, respectively, dominating the scene. The indigenous speech of Iztlan is uncertain, but Tecual (Tecualme), possibly a dialect of Huichol (concentrated in the mountain mass north of the Santiago River), prevailed in the other three provinces—although some Nahua was also in use. At the farthest end of the arc, near the northern edge of the southern Nayarit highland, the famous twin towns of Xalisco and Tepic headed rival provinces of considerable importance. The former spoke Tecual (called "Otomi" in the earliest records), the latter at least some Nahua. In spite of their renown, little is known about them beyond the fact that they were both quite warlike, particularly Xalisco, which put up a stiff resistance to Spanish domination. Considerable trade between the highland and lowland pueblos also characterized aboriginal southern Nayarit.

In general, it can be said that the native peoples of the arc where the shaft-chamber tomb cemeteries are concentrated exemplified a way of life which was typically Mesoamerican in its most essential aspects, particularly subsistence patterns. Lacking, however, were many of the more elaborate developments, especially in ceremonial art and architecture and in certain intellectual attainments (complex calendric and hieroglyphic writing

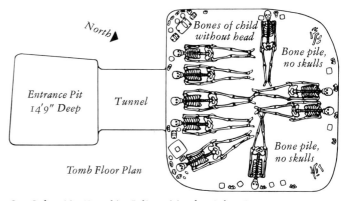

San Sebastián, Etzatlán, Jalisco, Tomb 1 (after Long 1966)

systems, books, etc.), of the nuclear Mesoamerican zones to the east. The area, as was true of almost all West Mexico west of the Tarascan imperium, was also characterized by a high degree of political fragmentation. Undoubtedly related to this was the considerable linguistic variety. All this is clearly reflected in the archaeological record, to which we now turn.

West Mexican Archaeology: General Considerations

Up to about the beginning of the Christian era, West Mexico appears to have shared with most of Mesoamerica the general pattern of village agriculture, perhaps introduced a few centuries earlier. However, about the period when such great Classic centers as Teotihuacán and Monte Albán were flowering and exerting powerful influences throughout extensive areas, in the west distinctive kinds of communities, art styles, and probably religions, prevailed. Proto-Classic and Classic Central Mexico, and other nuclear Mesoamerican regions were characterized by towns and small cities with ceremonial centers dominated by large mound constructions, often with stone and/or plaster facings, arranged around plazas; sculptured stone monuments; smaller carved items of jade and jade-like stones; and much outstanding religious art in general. West Mexico stands apart, for its communities were obviously smaller on the average, lacking very large mounds and sophisticated stone-plaster architecture. Although some kind of relatively simple religious architecture was undoubtedly present, perhaps even more important as ritual constructions were the shaft-chamber tombs. Higher level aesthetic expression was apparently largely concentrated on ceramic sculptures. Ritual practices may have centered on a cult of the dead, perhaps a kind of "ancestor worship," rather than on a complex hierarchy of powerful independent deities as was typical elsewhere in Classic Mesoamerica.

It was during this period of relative separation from the main currents of Classic Mesoamerican civilization that most of the pieces in the present exhibition were produced. The ceramic mortuary sculptures, especially, represent the apex of ancient West Mexican art, for other media—at least that which was imperishable—were little developed. The artistic energies and capabilities of the craftsmen of this region were seemingly channeled into the production of great quantities of ceramic figures and vessels designed to accompany the dead as mortuary offerings.

West Mexico was not entirely isolated from influences of the great Classic Mesoamerican civilizations to the east, particularly Teotihuacán, at least in Colima (Von Winning 1958; McBride and Delgado, ms.), but these influences do not seem to have been very substantial. Interestingly, the vigorous tradition of the shaft-chamber tombs and their elaborate ceramic offerings appears to fade out at about the same time (ca. A.D. 5th-6th centuries?) as that of the maximum spread of Teotihuacán influence. Whether these events were interrelated is perhaps questionable. At any rate, in the Early Postclassic, probably beginning about A.D. 800-900, considerable Toltec and Mixteca-Puebla influences effectively penetrated West Mexico, especially in the northwest. From this time forward the area obviously participates much more fully in pan-Mesoamerican developments. The distinctive local traditions in ceramic mortuary figures and vessels were absorbed or dominated by these eastern traditions, and the shaft-chamber tombs apparently were no longer constructed. Perhaps the introduction of new religious-ritual systems from the east, along with associated socioeconomic patterns, was responsible for the demise of the shaft-chamber tomb complex. Whatever the explanation, a unique cultural tradition passed into limbo. The art styles of the subsequent cultures of the area—even after contact with Central Mexico was again largely cut off by the rise of the Tarascan empire of Michoacán in the fifteenth century—lost much of their originality and creative freshness as they joined, as peripheral "country cousins," the larger aesthetic universe of Mesoamerica as a whole. A remarkable world had disappeared, leaving behind a rich legacy in the astounding quantity of fine ceramic pieces which now grace mantelpieces and museum cases throughout the globe.

The Shaft-Chamber Tombs: Available Physical Data

As has been pointed out, nearly all of the archaeological art objects of West Mexico have been recovered by local farmers and other persons hunting for saleable specimens. While it was known that most were found in tombs, until recently no professional archaeologist had actually excavated a completely undisturbed example of any importance. Little was known, therefore, of the precise way the figures were arranged in the mortuary chambers. Even more important, the age of the tombs and their contents was quite uncertain. Kelly's hypothesis, mentioned above, which equated the tomb period of Colima (Ortices) with Teotihuacán III, was accepted by many, but others suggested dates ranging from several hundred years before Christ to as late as the thirteenth century. Although Disselhoff (1932, 1960) and Corona Nuñez (1954, 1955) above all had contributed to a better understanding of the actual forms of the shaft-chamber tombs and the layouts of their contents, a more intensive kind of investigation was clearly indicated. This came in 1962-1964, with the UCLA Magdalena Basin (Etzatlán) Project, directed in the field by the late Stanley Long (Nicholson 1962; Long 1966; Long and Taylor 1966a).

The key tomb was San Sebastián 1, which provided detailed, generally reliable information concerning the interments and associated offerings. Long, in addition to inspecting carefully the original tomb, could analyze what survived of the bones of nine adult individuals (two males, seven females?), two fetuses, and nearly all of the objects removed from the single chamber. In addition to many pottery vessels and objects of shell and stone, no less than eighteen large hollow ceramic figures of men and women had been found, seventeen of which were available for study. These were of two distinct types, labeled by Long "San Sebastián Red" (7) and "El Arenal Brown" (10). The former affiliated with types commonly found in the Ahuacatlán valley, to the west in Nayarit, while the latter was a well-known "Jalisco" type. In itself, the presence of these two distinct types suggested to Long the possibility that this tomb—and probably others in the vicinity—were family crypts or had some other kind of periodic re-use. Since the San Sebastián Red figures consistently displayed a greater amount of manganese oxide patina, he deduced that they pre-dated the other type. Radiocarbon dates on three shells, obsidian hydration measurements of some of the obsidian artifacts, and ultra-violet fluorescence and organic nitrogen content analysis of the bones also tended to support the hypothesis of re-use. Accordingly, Long suggested the likelihood of at least three re-openings of the tomb and new interments following the original burial, extending over a period perhaps greater than 200 years, the last of which might have been a retainer burial (one male, four females). Others (e.g., Furst 1966) have questioned the re-use hypothesis, suggesting that diverse styles and types of objects were customarily assembled for single tomb interments (see also Taylor, ms.).

Long also investigated nine other shaft-chamber tombs in four other cemetery sites, making accurate diagrams, recovering various objects (both complete and fragmentary, including large ceramic figures) left behind or not discovered by the tomb robbers, photographing tomb pieces in private possession, and interrogating informants who were in a position to provide relevant information concerning the original loci of objects in the mortuary chambers. Some of these had contained a third major "Jalisco" type of large hollow figure which Long, following Kelly's suggestion, labeled "Ameca Gray." Because this type displayed features of both of the others, he suggested it occupied an intermediate temporal position between them.

It is now clear that the shaft-chamber tombs throughout the arc of their distribution vary greatly in size and form (see pages 18, 22, 24, 29). The shafts reach to a depth of at least 52 feet; the number of chambers varies from one to three. A short entrance passage almost invariably connects the chamber with the shaft. Most of the tombs were carved into *tepetate,* a water-deposited volcanic tuff. Stone slabs often cover the chamber entrances, and the shafts are usually filled up to the surface opening. That great effort was involved in their construction is clear from their depths and the care with which the chambers were hollowed out. According to Furst (1966: 269-272), some shaft-chamber tombs in southern Nayarit contain *claraboyas,* small shafts connecting chambers or a chamber with the surface (the latter for "feeding the dead"?). He also suggests that it is possible that a small shrine was erected over the tomb, where peri-odic ceremonies could have been held in honor of the ancestors below. He believes he has discerned possible traces of such constructions, particularly over Las Cebollas Tomb 1. There is now usually little or no surface indication of most of the tombs. However, since they usually occur in cemeteries containing from several to fifty or more, occasionally laid out in patterned alignments, once the first is located the diggers continue working in every direction until they have found all of the tombs in the cemetery. These cemeteries are usually located on elevations higher than the villages where the people lived. There is great variation in the tomb contents. Some have apparently been found empty or virtually so. The smaller ones sometimes contain only a few items. In others, particularly the multi-chambered examples, dozens of large hollow figures, vessels, and many shell and stone objects are found. There does not appear to be any very positive correlation between the richness of the offerings and the depth of the tomb, although it is unlikely that any over sixteen feet deep was not provided with important objects.

The exact spatial distribution of the shaft-chamber tomb sites remains to be plotted in detail. They seem to be almost continuously distributed through the oft-mentioned Nayarit-Jalisco-Colima arc (see page 8). The northern boundary is fuzzy. They may extend as far north as southern Sinaloa (cf. Furst 1966: 208), but this has never been absolutely verified. The eastern boundary is also somewhat indeterminate; they certainly extend almost to Guadalajara, if not beyond. Aside from the special case of El Opeño, and possibly just across the Colima border along the lower Río Coahuayana, they apparently have not been found in Michoacán. On the west, they extend to the coastal plain, at least in the Ameca Valley, but they are obviously rare there. Certainly the great concentration is in the inland, mostly highland arc between Colima and the Tepic area of Nayarit.

The whole shaft-chamber tomb complex is essentially alien to Mesoamerica, and—with one partial exception, the small *"sótanos"* of the Mixteca Alta of northwestern Oaxaca (Bernal 1948-1949), which are much later in time (Late Postclassic)—are found nowhere except in the area just delineated. Following up the stimulating discussions of Corona Nuñez (1955), Noguera (1955), Furst (1966, 1967), and others, Long (1967) in an important paper plotted the New World distribution of this type of subterranean mortuary structure and set up a comprehensive typology. They are most common and most elaborate in northwestern South America, particularly in Colombia and Ecuador. Since the South American tombs occasionally also contain large hollow figures (usually quite different in style, however, from the Mexican ones), some archaeologists have speculated that there may have been some direct connection between the shaft-chamber tomb complexes of the two areas. Although such historical linkages are not presently demonstrable, they remain an intriguing possibility for future investigation (Meighan 1969).

The principal alternative origin hypothesis would derive the

West Mexican tradition from Preclassic Central Mexico via Chupícuaro (Porter 1956, 1969; McBride 1969) and El Opeño. There are undeniable resemblances in the ceramics of these areas on an early time horizon. Such a derivation, however, would still leave the shaft-chamber tombs themselves unaccounted for since they are lacking in Central Mexico, including the Chupícuaro area of northeastern Michoacán-south Guanajuato. In any case, it is clear that both the tombs and their contents were quite distinct from the mortuary patterns contemporaneously prevailing in the rest of Mesoamerica. Some explanation must be sought for the unique and vital tomb-excavating cultures which flourished in West Mexico during this early period.

Although not all the shaft-chamber tombs are of great depth, it does appear that most of the ceramic mortuary offerings of the type featured in this exhibition are found within them. The deep ones obviously required considerable time to dig and prepare. The modern tomb robbers take a week or so to excavate a deep tomb, and the original digging must have taken much longer since the ancient workmen had no metal shovels or picks (and perhaps worked only with pointed sticks and/or stone picks to break up the earth). It seems likely that the larger tombs were prepared in advance of the death, and, as previously mentioned, it is also possible that, in some cases at least, the tombs were re-used and served as family crypts. However, since individual burials occur in simpler and shallower graves, it is clear that not everyone in the community was accorded the elaborate ritual of a shaft-chamber tomb burial. The larger tombs were probably constructed for leading, upper-class families, not only because of the great effort required to prepare the tomb but also because of the abundance of elaborate offerings they usually contain.

The Mortuary Offerings:
Regional-Temporal Traditions and Types

The mortuary offerings found in the shaft-chamber tombs consist, aside from human and animal skeletal remains, of both ceramic and non-ceramic objects. The latter include numerous ornaments and other objects of shell and, occasionally, bone (e.g., trumpets; necklaces; armlets and bracelets; nose- and earrings; pectorals; and *atlatl* finger-loops) and stone (e.g., *metates* and *manos*, axes; obsidian cores, flakes, scrapers, blades, points, and "mirrors"; slate "mirrors" and encrusted pyrites; necklaces; pectorals; and small anthropomorphic and zoomorphic images). Objects of other materials (cloth, feathers, wood, basketry, and matting) and foodstuffs and liquids also undoubtedly were placed in the tomb chambers, but these have not survived.

The most important objects from an archaeological and artistic standpoint are the ceramic pieces, on which the following discussion will concentrate. These consist principally of anthropomorphic and zoomorphic figures (a few represent inanimate objects), both hollow and solid (the former usually much

larger), and vessels. Especially in Colima, the large hollow figures also often served as vessels; sometimes the vessels display figures modeled on their surfaces.

No comprehensive typology of West Mexican ceramic mortuary pieces has yet been published, nor will it be our purpose in this brief article to undertake one.[3] A few general remarks must suffice. Certain broad distinctions have long been generally accepted, particularly the basic tripartite division into "Nayarit," "Jalisco," and "Colima" traditions (although the last two have often been merged). They share certain modes, such as the "shoulder knobs" (cicatrices?), which are occasionally even encountered on Chupícuaro figures. Within each of these major traditions various finer typological subdivisions have been recognized, but much remains to be done along this line—beyond the pioneer efforts of Toscano (1946), Kirchhoff (1946), Kelly (1948, 1949), Gifford (1950), Kubler (1962), Long (1966), and others.

Beginning with Colima, certain gross categories are immediately apparent: 1) the large hollow anthropomorphic and zoomorphic figures (often effigy vessels), most commonly of slipped and polished redware (Nos. 106, 107, 109, 110, 111, 112, 113, 114, 115, 116, 117, 118, 119, 120, 121, 122, 123, 124, 125, 126, 129, 131, 133, 134, 151, 152, 153, 156, 192, 198 [skeuomorphs of inanimate objects], 154, 157, 159, 161, 163, 164, 165, 166, 167, 170, 171, 173, 175, 176, 177); 2) large, flattish solid anthropomorphic figures, both slipped and unslipped (132, 135, 141, 144); 3) with no sharp division from the last category, smaller, usually unslipped figures (including zoomorphs), commonly whistles (136, 137, 138, 140, 142, 143, 145, 146, 147 A-O, 172, 174) often performing various activities (dancers and other ritual performers, warriors in full regalia, acrobats, women performing household chores and tending babies, musicians, etc.) sometimes (e.g., dance groups and figures on palanquins carried by bearers) in joined groups but more often individual, or paired (see Kelly 1949: 111-124, for a useful discussion of southern Jalisco-Colima figurines of these two types); 4) rather abstract masks (148, 150); 5) miscellaneous musical instruments: whistles, flutes, ocarinas, rattles (201), skeuomorphs of conch shell trumpets and drums, etc. (see Kunike 1912; Van Giffen-Duyvis 1959); 6) "house groups" (rare, and usually with no accompanying figures); 7) an unslipped "grotesque" type of anthropomorphic "Janus" *incensario* with loop handles (199; Postclassic?; see discussion of this type in Disselhoff 1960); 8) "simple" vessels (190, 191), with unsupported *olla*, jar, and bowl forms predominating but also including various "exotic" and "abstract" forms (108, 183, 185, 186, 194, 195, 197), usually monochrome (sometimes incised or engraved) but occasionally bi- and polychrome); 9) vessels with effigy "additions," both anthropomorphic, especially rows of heads (127, 128), and zoomorphic (165, 169); 10) globular vessels, usually somewhat flattened, often ribbed, with zoomorphic (especially parrots) or anthropomorphic tripod supports (188, 189); and 11) phytomorphic vessels (178, 179, 180, 181, 182,

184, 193), almost invariably monochrome.

Within certain of these broad categories (a selective, not exhaustive, list) many subtypes can be distinguished, based on various criteria: formal qualities, especially configuration of the eyes, posture, costume, activities portrayed, if any, etc. Worth special mention are the phallic figures (Nos. 115, 147 C, D, E), apparently unique to Colima, and, among the inanimate objects represented, the strange aviform *reclinatorios* (backrests: 111, 147 F, L, M). Some of these subtypes undoubtedly have chronological implications, but, without the control of systematic excavations, seriations based wholly on removed pieces must be considered quite tentative, however "logical."

The range of zoomorphic representations (including grotesques, double-headed [No. 170], merged [157], etc.) is especially remarkable. Aside from the famous dogs (147 B, 152, 153, 154, 156), most of the animals prominent in the environment are represented: deer, jaguar, peccary, monkey, coati (155), squirrel, gopher (161), mouse (167), armadillo, frog-toad (164, 168), bat, various types of lizards (159, 164, 169), turtle (162), snake (170), fish (165), crab (163), lobster, shrimp, and various birds—parrot (175), duck (176) and other aquatics (171, 173), turkey (173), owl (77), swallow, etc. The phytomorphic vessels also represent a broad range of plants, especially cacti and food plants (particularly fruits); precise botanical identifications, however, are often difficult. The non-effigy pottery vessels exhibit considerable variety in form and decoration. Only a beginning (see, especially, Kelly 1949) has been made in working out a comprehensive typology for those types found in the tombs and burials and the non-mortuary types contemporary with them.

As indicated, various subtypes within the "Jalisco" figure tradition of the Magdalena Basin and adjoining territory have been proposed by Long (1966), who suggested they are sequent (but probably with some overlap): San Sebastián Red (Nos. 25, 54, 55, 56, 58, 59, 60, 61, 62, 63, 64, 65, 66, 69)—plus Ojos Variant (57, 67, for the purposes of this exhibition classified with the "Nayarit" tradition); Ameca Gray (74, 75, 76, 81, 82, 83, 84, 95, 99); and El Arenal Brown (86, 89, 98). In contrast to Colima, where painted decoration of figures is rare, they are frequently decorated in complex layouts, including much resist or negative painting. Other types from this same general region, including various smaller solid varieties (90, 91, 92, 93, 94, 101, 102, 104), are also quite apparent but have yet to be assigned specific labels. Examples are a particularly long-faced type (87) attributed (e.g., Parres Arias 1962) to San Juanito, also in the Magdalena Basin (municipio of Antonio Escobedo), and a distinctive type (unrepresented in the exhibition; for typical examples see Gifford 1950: Pl. 2d; Parres Arias 1963b, 1965b; Marks 1968: 15, upper left) painted in white with elongated heads, headbands or turbans, round ear spools, and usually rather "pointed" ears and facial features, some examples of which have been attributed to the Guadalajara region. A more generalized "type," characterized by a gray-brown slip—sometimes featur-

ing figures with enormous legs—also appears to belong to this broad "Jalisco" division (96, 97, 100, 105).

In general, these "Jalisco" figures display less variety of form and activity than those of Colima and Nayarit. They are often quite large in size. Male-female pairs, sometimes joined, are known (No. 84). Probably the most striking single representation is "the armed warrior" (86), often with helmet (sometimes bicorn) and armor, and club, mace, or stabbing spear. It cross-cuts Long's types, although it is rare in El Arenal Brown. Animals are uncommon in this tradition—and then usually only the dog (70, 71, 72) occurs, here classified as "Nayarit." Whether "house groups" are present is doubtful; if so, they are extremely rare. Although he described in detail many complete or fragmentary vessels from the tombs, Long did not attempt a systematic typology. The unsupported bowl is the commonest form, often decorated in bichrome and polychrome abstract and stylized design layouts, including those applied with the resist technique.

The "Nayarit" (often called "Ixtlán del Río") types are, like those of Colima, quite diversified (which again may reflect temporal differences). Large hollow and small solid anthropomorphic and zoomorphic figures predominate. The latter (confined mostly to the dog [Nos. 9, 29] and frog-toad [10]) are quite rare. The quantity and variety of the former, on the other hand, is remarkable. The San Sebastián Red type can also be placed within the broad "Nayarit" tradition (and is almost invariably so assigned); it can perhaps best be designated "Nayarit-Jalisco." The addition of painted decoration is also common here, particularly designs (including resist) in white, yellow, and black. Male-female pairs, separate or joined, are particularly common in this tradition (14, 18, 19, 21, 22). The larger human figures exhibit a wide range of variation as regards "realism." Some often strike modern observers as virtually amounting to caricatures (e.g., 14, 16, 18, 19), while others are subtly modeled in a much more "naturalistic" mode (e.g., 12, 15, 21, 22). There are many gradations, making it difficult to divide them sharply into two distinct categories. The so-called "Chinesco" group (1, 2, 3, 4, 5, 6, 7, 11) has to be broken down into various sub-categories, although they merge into one another in a rather complex fashion.

Here also the "armed warrior," often with a bicorn helmet, is common. Another frequent male headdress—on "armed warrior" as well as other types of figures—is conical or peaked, often with a kind of heavy fringe depending over the forehead (Nos. 12, 14, 15, 16, 28, 35). The twisted turban is worn by both sexes (18). Headbands, however, are the commonest headgears (e.g., 19). Diseased and emaciated figures (e.g., 24, 43; see Ramón Meza, 1960, Anonymous 1965) are frequent, as are those, both male and female, exhibiting remarkable mutilation patterns, usually parallel groups of slits, on the cheeks and around the mouth (e.g., in the Nayarit-Jalisco San Sebastián Red type, 63, 64, 65). An extraordinary penitential "joining" ritual involves groups of such figures (20, 23). Some features of costume and ornamentation are particularly characteristic of the Nayarit tradition, e.g., the short-sleeved male shirt not quite reaching to the crotch (e.g., 12, 15); a similar garment, somewhat longer, was worn by the historic Tarascans of Michoacán); very short trousers with "scoop loincloth," also worn by males (e.g., 14, 16); a small mantle tied over one shoulder with cords—in contrast to the mantle knotted over one shoulder in the rest of Mesoamerica (e.g., 19); the female loincloth (21, 24); the curved or angular nose bar (16, 18); and noserings and earrings in profusion (12, 14, 15, 18, 19, 24).

The complex scenes involving numerous small solid human and animal figures (e.g., Nos. 26, 31, 33, 36), particularly the "house groups" (27, 30, 38; see Borhegyi 1964; Lehmann 1964; Von Winning 1959, ms.), the ballcourt scenes (34), the "funeral processions" (e.g., Von Winning and Stendahl 1969; Pls. 156, 157), the "pole ritual" (35), and the battle scenes (e.g., Von Winning and Stendahl 1969: Pl. 154), constitute an especially striking type within the Nayarit tradition. In their detail and elaboration there is really nothing fully comparable to them in the entire pre-European New World. Their ethnographic value is enormous. The most common forms of vessels associated with the figures are unsupported bowls, jars, and *ollas,* but more complex shapes (e.g., 45, 46), including tripod vessels, are also known. Bichrome and polychrome painted decoration (including resist) is common. Gifford (1950) has worked out a preliminary typology for Early Ixtlán, based on surface-collected and stolen pieces, which will be refined on the basis of stratigraphic excavations in the future.

Of interest is the question of whether the tomb offerings were made specifically to be buried with the dead or whether they were household possessions which saw some use prior to their placement in the mortuary chambers. This question is not answerable in detail, but some of the tomb pieces show definite signs of wear and must have been used prior to their tomb deposition. It is not impossible that the human ceramic figures represented specific individuals, perhaps including ancestors. They might have been kept in the homes of the people—or even in shrines—until their use in a mortuary ritual.

Virtually nothing is known of the villages occupied by the excavators of the tombs, and these suggestions cannot be verified or disproved until the settlements as well as the cemetery areas are carefully investigated. The deepest and most elaborate shaft-chamber tombs were probably prepared during the lifetime of the individuals to be buried there, as in ancient Egypt and in other early cultures which placed great stress on mortuary ritual and a continued life in the afterworld.

Ethnographic-Iconographic Interpretations

Finally, we come to the problem of ethnographic and iconographic interpretations, a complicated and difficult topic which can only be outlined briefly here. In general, it can be said that the great ethnographic value of these mortuary offerings is so obvious as to almost constitute a cliché. They illustrate a wide range of sociocultural patterns (although important sectors of the culture are not depicted), more so certainly than any other Mesoamerican tradition (only approached by the Gulf Coast cultures and that of the makers of the Jaina figurines). In the pre-European New World, probably only the Moche-Chimu tradition, North Coast Peru, provides a more complete cultural "ceramic picture book." A partial list of principal topics portrayed would include: physical appearance of the population, clothing, and ornamentation (including mutilations and effects of disease); many tools, weapons, and other artifacts; dwellings and probably ceremonial and other structures and activities within or associated with them, including food preparation and child care; rituals (including funerals and possibly weddings) and games; military activities; and wild and domestic animals and plants in their environment (mostly confined to Colima).

One of the most difficult questions concerning the interpretation of the West Mexican mortuary ceramic figures is whether genuine supernatural beings are represented. Considerable differences of opinion prevail here. Most students (e.g., Toscano 1946; Kirchhoff 1946; Covarrubias 1957) have emphasized the "secular," non-religious orientation of this art, at times flatly affirming that no deities or even deity-impersonators are represented. Certainly ritual performers (dancers, both masked and unmasked, phallic performers, musicians in what is probably a ritual context, etc.) are depicted and, quite possibly, religious practitioners (priests, shamans; e.g., No. 116?) as well. Whether any particular figure actually represented a clear-cut image of a discrete deity as such, an "idol" if you will, is perhaps

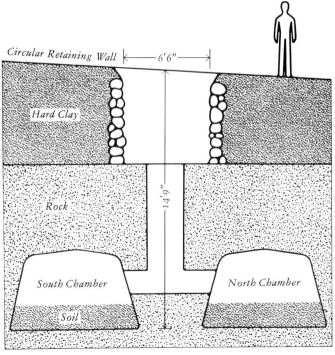

Las Cebollas, seen from east side, Tequilita, Nayarit,
Tomb 1 (after Delgado 1969)

Circular Retaining Wall ⟵ 6'6" ⟶

Hard Clay

Rock

14'9"

South Chamber   North Chamber

Soil

doubtful.[4] In this connection it might be worth noting that among the thousands of Mesoamerican Preclassic clay figurines (even Olmec and Olmecoid) very few can be interpreted positively as depictions of specific deities. Not until Classic times does this appear to have become common, especially in Oaxaca, and it is precisely during the Classic that West Mexico appears to have been most isolated from direct influences from the remainder of Mesoamerica.

This discussion inevitably leads to the most fundamental question of all: what was the specific purpose and function of these ceramic figures? Why were they placed in the tombs and burials? Unfortunately, with no concrete ethnohistoric data to guide us, speculation must rule. Some (e.g., Toscano 1946) have suggested that these figures, supernaturally vivified, were thought to continue their earthly existence in the afterlife. In this view they would have represented both the deceased (the diseased figures representing the fatal illness?) and his/her retainers (spouse or spouses, servants, etc.; as indicated above, there is a possibility that retainer sacrifice and interment was a feature of the mortuary complex associated with shaft-chamber tombs). As Toscano pointed out, since hunchbacks and other deformed persons were a standard fixture of the palace retinues of late pre-Hispanic Central Mexican rulers, the hunchback figures (particularly common in Colima; e.g., No. 134) might lend this hypothesis some support. So might also the figures ("palace" servants and/or slaves?) carrying various objects with the tumpline, which are frequent in Colima (e.g., 111, 112, 120, 126). Along this same line, Toscano also linked the Colima dog figures with the late pre-Hispanic Central Mexican custom of slaying the deceased's dog, who was believed to ferry his master's soul across the River of the Underworld to his final resting place on the other side. Again, it might be pertinent to mention that the precise function of most Preclassic and Classic Mesoamerican figurines (often placed in graves; e.g., Tlatilco, Jaina, etc.) is also quite uncertain. This problem of the specific purpose of ceramic figures, therefore, is by no means confined to West Mexico.

One basic ethnographic interpretation, particularly for Colima, seems quite likely (cf. Kirchhoff 1946). These societies must have been characterized by some significant degree of stratification, with an elite group possessing considerable power and prestige. The mere existence of deep shaft-chamber tombs with as many as three carefully constructed chambers would suggest a considerable degree of social differentiation. The great expenditure of time and labor necessary to construct such elaborate mortuary chambers would most likely have been expended particularly on behalf of members of an important upper class (particularly the members of ruling dynasties) rather than for every member of these societies. Furthermore, the palanquins of Colima (e.g., No. 138), borne by four to eight bearers, evidence clear cut class-status distinctions—as perhaps do the male figures, often holding what appears to be fans (a badge of rank elsewhere in Mesoamerica), leaning back against the strange

aviform *reclinatorios* (147 F, L). The same might hold for the "umbrellas" (e.g., 6), and as Kirchoff has suggested, four-footed stools, on which males are seated (130) may also have been rank indicators as in other parts of Mesoamerica (e.g., Tarascan Michoacán, Tlaxcala and neighboring provinces) and the aboriginal New World. What appear to be elaborate Nayarit funeral processions also point the same way. A high social position for at least some women is also suggested by various data, above all their presence alongside male figures on Colima palanquins (e.g., México, Secretaría de Educación Pública 1946: Pl. 81). The large, complex two-story houses of some of the Nayarit "house groups" could be additional indicators of rank-status differences (residences of rulers?), as well as the considerable variations in elaborateness of attire of figures within the same tradition.

Certain classes of figures have given rise to various "obvious" interpretations, based on appearances, such as the "armed warriors," the "ball players" (male figures holding balls: No. 13), the "mourners" (seated figures, often emaciated, leaning their heads on their arms; e.g., 54, 55, 56, 57, 58, 62), the "musicians" (playing various instruments; e.g., 5, 14, 25, 26, 106, 109, 147 D, M, N, O), the "imbibers" (apparently sucking up liquids with tubes from vessels; e.g., 18?), the "dancers" (in animated poses, often masked and/or wearing elaborate costumes; e.g., 114, 116, 147 A, C, D, E?), the "acrobats" (119, 121, 137), and various others. Some of these "obvious" (i.e., obvious from the standpoint of a participant in modern Western culture) interpretations may well be legitimate; others probably are not.

To take one representative example, an alternative explanation which has been suggested for the "mourners" is that such figures rather depict individuals in a narcotic trance from peyote or some other hallucinogenic drug. Among the contemporary Huichol, persons in a peyote trance do sit in the same way as these figures. Since peyote is a sacred plant of the deepest religious import, used as a means of passage to the spirit world, such a figure would be highly appropriate in the tombs of individuals involved in a peyote cult type of religion. At the time of the Conquest, the peyote cult was particularly flourishing among the groups located mostly north and east of the Río Grande de Santiago, known to the Central Mexicans as "Teochichimeca"; they apparently included the Cora, Huichol, Tepecano, Cazcan, Zacateca, Guamares, Cuachachil, and their neighbors. Whether this cult can be projected back many centuries and to another area located somewhat to the south is perhaps questionable. The characteristic peyote cactus bud may be represented in Colima ceramics, but this is not certain.

This is an example of an interpretation largely derived from "ethnographic analogy," in this case invoking a ritual pattern among a group, the Huichol, who live in an area not too far removed from the ancient tomb arc and much of whose culture, above all in its religious-ritual aspect, has survived remarkably intact. Furst (1965c, d, 1966) has particularly emphasized ethnographic analogy in interpreting the significance of West

Mexican mortuary figures, at times throwing out a virtually global net, especially in his interpretation of the "horned" Colima "warriors" as shamans (invariably, he maintains, depicted with a sinistral orientation) with "horns of power." He even cites at length the observations of modern Huichol medicine men when shown these figures or their photographs. Although this vigorous use of ethnographic analogy may direct our thinking to some interpretations which are plausible, such a procedure is somewhat hazardous when we attempt to project back hundreds of years the culture patterns of any contemporary group, however closely continguous geographically they may be to the archaeological zone in question. If employed with critical caution, however, as one means of generating hypotheses, this approach has undeniable value—and it has been used to good advantage from the beginning of systematic archaeology in both hemispheres.

However, it is one thing to admit the likelihood that some of the mortuary figures, particularly some of the Colima figures, represent religious practitioners (shamans or priests; these societies were probably on a sufficient level of complexity to have had the latter, as elsewhere in Mesoamerica). It is quite another to interpret all of the single horned Colima figures and the double-horned "Nayarit" and "Nayarit-Jalisco" ones who display obvious martial attributes as "shamans whose frequently explicit fighting stance is related not to any earthly warfare, but to the supernatural struggle against underworld demons threatening the deceased" (Furst 1965c; 60). Whatever the precise significance of the horn(s), we feel that the more "obvious" interpretation of these figures as indeed secular warriors in fighting gear is at least as likely as the hypothesis that they represented "shamanic guardians of the dead."

Another interesting example of the use of ethnographic analogy to interpret a certain type of figure found frequently in the tombs is that of Delgado (1969), who explains the so-called "babe in cradle" figures (e.g., Nos. 101, 102) as representing corpses on biers prepared for burial. He notes as analogy modern mortuary practice in a mestizo town (descended from a native Cazcan or Nahua-speaking community), Ajijic, on the north shore of Lake Chapala, Jalisco. Some details which are consistent with such an interpretation include the projections on either side of the head, which are hardly a pillow or headrest but may be intended to hold the head in place, and the fact that the figures are tied to the platform with bands across the body. Weisman (Anonymous 1965), on the other hand, interprets these as "figures lying on primitive hospital beds," Lehmann (1951, 1953) agrees that they are sick persons being treated by curing shamans, while Morss (1952) holds the view that they indeed represent infants lashed to cradle boards.

These differences of opinion are typical of the problems encountered in attempting to arrive at solid, convincing explanations of the meaning, purpose and function of many of the West Mexican mortuary ceramic pieces. To cite another obvious example, how are the Colima biomorphic figures (apart from the dogs) to be interpreted? Toscano (1946) suggested that the animal figures depicted the *nahual*, the "guardian spirit" or "companion animal" of the deceased. But some of the animals, especially the maritime ones, do not seem to qualify particularly well for such a role, not to mention the problem of the group representations (especially pairs and trios of ducks [e.g., No. 176]). Most are also vessels and may have contained foods and liquids placed in the mortuary chambers to accompany the deseased to the afterworld. Precisely why they represent these particular animals and birds, however, is undeniably obscure.

Other figures for which an interpretation based on ethnographic analogy might be suggested are the paired couples: a man and a woman modeled as a single piece of ceramic sculpture, particularly characteristic of Nayarit (e.g., Nos. 14, 19). In terms of our own culture patterns these could be (and often are) interpreted as marriage scenes. On the other hand, these pairs could well represent ritual performances of some kind. The man often holds what appears to be a rattle; the woman characteristically holds a small bowl or cup in one hand and usually has her arm around the male figure. They may be scenes of a man singing and chanting, the woman holding an offering (or perhaps some narcotic to be taken by the man).

While our understanding of the precise meaning of the figures must remain fragmentary and uncertain, our appreciation of them as art objects is enhanced by even a partial understanding of what may have been in the mind of the artist at the time he was creating the dramatic and expressive images seen in the exhibition. The detailed interpretations are still to be worked out, but the purpose of these pieces seems most likely to be related at least in part to their makers' religious-ritual practices. This treatment of ethnographic-iconographic interpretations could be greatly extended, but space limitations do not allow further discussion. Sufficient examples have been adduced to illustrate the problems and challenges inherent in this type of analysis.

Concluding Observations

The foregoing discussion, while too brief to cover all aspects of the rich, complex archaeology of West Mexico, should at least provide some general notion of where we appear to stand today in our knowledge of the period of the shaft-chamber tombs and contemporaneous burials of Nayarit, Jalisco, and Colima. This exhibition, the first major exhibition in the United States dedicated solely to aesthetically superior pieces from the West Mexican cemeteries, provides an excellent cross-section of the creative genius of a group of culturally related peoples whose very existence had apparently been long forgotten when the Europeans first reached the area. Only in relatively modern times have the remarkable objects they placed in such profusion in their tombs and burials been extracted in quantity and exposed to the curious, not fully-comprehending, scrutiny of collectors, museum visitors, and oft-puzzled scholars. Largely in this century, a whole lost world of ancient America has been suddenly revealed. No hieroglyphic texts or even oral traditions are available to aid in the reconstruction of their histories or their beliefs. Only careful archaeological analysis of all extant mortuary and domestic pieces, combined with additional field investigations, can further our understanding of these long-vanished tomb excavators and extraordinarily gifted artists. Luckily, the essentially realistic depiction in durable fired clay of their cultural and natural world provides us with unique reconstructive opportunities. Much has been done, but much remains to be done. It is hoped that this exhibition and the accompanying catalog will add significantly to our knowledge and appreciation of some of the most interesting and intensively alive cultures that flourished in this hemisphere.

Notes

1 All available radiocarbon dates from Trans-Tarascan West Mexico, including those from the tomb cemetery sites, were recently (Taylor, Berger, Meighan, and Nicholson 1969) listed together and discussed. A few could now be added to that list, including one which apparently dates a late tomb phase. Comala, from La Loma (Los Amoles), Colima, at A.D. 500 (see Fig. 3).

2 Although not directly concerned with the problem of the tombs and their contents, UCLA's 1960-1962 coastal (mouth of Río Grande de Santiago to Río Balsas delta) surveys and excavations along the West Coast (Meighan 1961; Nicholson and Smith 1962; Nicholson 1963; Long and Wire 1966), particularly the excavation of the Morett Site, near Manzanillo, Colima (Meighan, ms.), added substantially to our knowledge of West Mexican archaeology (publication of this project is in progress). Especially relevant to the present topic are the data from the Morett Site, where a series of radiocarbon dates (Taylor, Berger, Meighan, and Nicholson 1969; 25-27) confirmed a very early occupation (beginning ca. 300 B.C.?). Morett ceramic types also display numerous cross-ties to those of the earliest Colima-southern Jalisco phases worked out by Kelly, particularly Tuxcacuesco.

3 Hasso Von Winning is presently engaged in a comprehensive analysis of the West Mexican mortuary ceramic figures which will include a systematic typological classification.

4 A Colima effigy piece (Von Winning and Stendahl 1969: Pl. 83) represents a kind of grotesque face, probably a mask (cf. 114), which displays features vaguely resembling those of Ehecatl, the wind god of various late Mesoamerican cultures — but this similarity could just be fortuitous.

Radiocarbon Dates: West Mexican Shaft—Chamber Tombs

LABORATORY NUMBER	SITE	SAMPLE MATERIAL	C14 AGE (corrected*)	ARCHAEOLOGICAL ASSOCIATIONS
UCLA 1012	Las Cebollas, Tequilita, Nayarit	Caribbean species marine shell	A.D. 100	Tomb containing "chinesco" ceramic figures, vessels, etc.
UCLA 593-A	San Sebastián Etzatlán Jalisco	Caribbean species marine shell	140 B.C.	
UCLA 593-B	"	Pacific species marine shell	120 B.C.	Tomb containing both San Sebastián Red ("Nayarit-Jalisco") and El Arenal Brown ("Jalisco") ceramic figures, vessels, etc.
UCLA 593-C	"	"	A.D. 400	
UCLA 966	"	Bone collagen	A.D. 300	
UCLA 1032	"	"	A.D. 335	
UCLA 1066	Chanchopa, Tecomán, Colima	Pacific species marine shell	A.D. 100	Tomb containing offertory pieces of the Ortices phase

*Pacific shell dates corrected for ocean upwelling; bone dates tree-ring calibrated.
Additional Colima tomb dates (which generally concur with those presented above) are being processed by the UCLA Isotope Laboratory and will be published in the future.

NAYARIT

1 LEFT: Smiling Woman, Nayarit, "Chinesco" style. Nude, wearing waistband, necklace, earrings, and noserings; orange-red slip with black and white painted decorations. One of the largest known of these distinctive "realistic Chinesco" figures (cf. very similar pieces illustrated in *Fondo de la Plástica Mexicana* 1964: Pl. 44; Furst 1966: Pls. 4-11). H. 24″ W. 15″ D. 12″

2 Seated Man, Nayarit, "Chinesco" style. Arms resting on up-raised knees, light cream slip with red slip on upper torso and lower legs, black painted decoration on face, hair, and indicating loincloth. Wears red and white headband, single armband, and nose plug. This piece is quite similar to the first "Chinesco" figure ever published (Lumholtz 1902, vol. 2: 294), attributed to Jalisco, Nayarit. H. 12″ W. 9″ D. 7½″

2

3 Seated Nude, Nayarit, "Chinesco" style. Female figure, red and light cream slip, black painted decoration on lower body, legs spread, hands on hips, wearing earrings, noserings, necklace, armbands, and waistbands in low relief. Unusually large example of this type. Although also popularly labeled "Chinesco" this type, commonly found in the area inland from San Blas, is distinct from Nos. 1 and 2 with a more rectangular head and hair carefully indicated by striations. Cf. 4, 7.
H. 23" W. 14" D. 12½"

4 Seated Nude, Nayarit, "Chinesco" style. Female figure, legs spread, wearing earrings and necklace, grayish cream slip with red slipped upper body and lower legs, supporting red slipped vessel on head. Cf. 3, 7.
(Published: Von Winning and Stendahl 1969: Pl. 164)
H. 9" W. 7½" D. 4¼"

5 Drummer, Nayarit, "Chinesco" style. Musician playing large gourd drum, white and black on burnished reddish-brown slip, wearing turban-like headdress with dependent bands trailing over shoulders, arm and leg bands, and loincloth. (Published: Von Winning and Stendahl 1969: Pl. 173)
H. 5½" W. 2½" D. 5½"

6 Seated Nude, "Chinesco style," Nayarit. Female figure wearing earrings, nose ornament and waistband. White painted decorations on burnished red slip; considerable black patina. A good example, somewhat more realistic than some, of a recognized "Chinesco" sub-type often referred to as "Martian Chinesco" (cf. Alsberg 1968: Fig. 47).
H. 8¼" W. 5¼" D. 5¾"

7 RIGHT: Seated Nude, Nayarit, "Chinesco" style. Female figure with legs spread, wearing earrings and necklace, red and light cream slips with resist decoration on lower body. Cf. 3, 4.
H. 16" W. 15" D. 9"

3

4

5

6

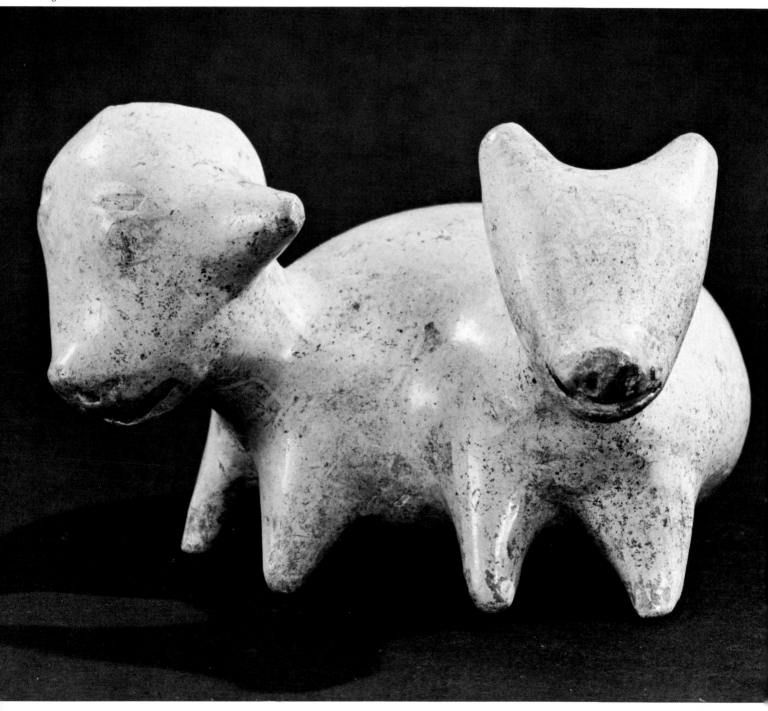

8 Double-Headed Dog, Nayarit, "Chinesco" style. Burnished white slip.
H. 3¼" W. 5" D. 5"

9 Dog, Nayarit, "Chinesco" style. White on red slip.
H. 7" W. 5½" D. 10"

10 Toad, Nayarit, "Chinesco" style (?). White painted decorations on burnished orange slip. Prominent vessel spout on back. Cf. identical Rivera collection piece illustrated in México, Secretaría de Educación Pública 1946: Pl. 41.
H. 5" L. 5½" W. 4"

11 "Contemplation," Nayarit, "Chinesco" style. Kneeling female nude, supporting hands and chin on raised knee; light cream slip with red slip on upper torso and lower legs, black painted decoration on lower body; wearing earrings, noserings, armlets, and waistband.
H. 13" W. 10½" D. 12"

12 Warrior in Patterned Shirt, Nayarit. Holding fan (?) and club or baton, wearing sleeveless shirt, pointed headdress, armlets, earrings, noseplug, and necklace; red slipped, black and white painted decorations on face and garments .
H. 31" W. 15" D. 9"

13 "Ballplayer," Nayarit. Seated, wearing serrated nose ornament, earrings, armlets, necklace, short-sleeved shirt, and short trousers with "scoop loincloth," holding ball in right hand. White and black painted decoration on red slip.
H. 18¼" W. 10" D. 9½"

9

10

11

12

13

14 LEFT: "The Conversation I," Nayarit. Joined couple, seated woman holding vessel, wearing "turban," earrings, noserings, crescentic pectoral, armlets, and skirt (with black, white, and yellow decoration on red slip); man wearing pointed conical headdress and virtually same ornaments as woman — plus trunks with "scoop loincloth" and "off-shoulder mantle." Cf.19.
H. 20½" W. 15" D. 11"

15 Man Wearing Fringed Hat, Nayarit. Holding small flat plate (tortilla?), wearing short-sleeved shirt, pointed woven headdress with "fringe," armlets, earrings, noserings, and necklace (cf. 12). Red and black slip.
H. 19" W. 11" D. 9"

16 Warrior and Mate (No. 17), Nayarit. Warrior holding spear-thrower (atlatl; cf. Lumholtz 1902, Vol. 2: Pl. v, a), wearing short-sleeved shirt, short trousers with "scoop loincloth," conch shell "belt buckle," pointed headdress with "fringe," armlets, earrings, necklace, and crescentic pectoral and nose ornament. Red-slipped, white and yellow painted decorations on headdress and garments.
H. 24" W. 11" D. 8"

17 Woman holding receptacle in right hand, wearing thick striped headband, nosering, earrings, armlets, necklace, crescentic pectoral, and skirt, white and black painted decorations on red slip.
H. 20½" W. 13" D. 6"

18 The Meal, Nayarit. Seated man with vessel and drinking tube (tamal? taco?), wearing twisted "turban," nose crescent, earrings, necklace, armlets, and loincloth.
H. 8" W. 4½" D. 4½"

Seated woman grinding maize on a metate (masa being pushed into vessel?), wearing twisted "turban," noserings, earrings, armlets, necklace, and skirt. White and black painted details on red slip.
H. 8" W. 4½" D. 4½"

19 "The Conversation II," Nayarit. Joined couple, seated, attired as 14, except that the male lacks the pointed headdress and holds a vessel instead of playing a drum. Red-slipped with white painted decorations (traces of black).
H. 13½" W. 9" D. 5½"

15

16

17

18

19

20 "Ceremonial Dance I," Nayarit. A female, wearing skirt, flanked by two nude males joined by rod thrust through cheeks — woman wearing earrings and nosering, men the same plus headbands; red, black, and yellow painted decoration on cream slip. This extraordinary penitential ritual, unreported for any other area of Mesoamerica, is undoubtedly connected with the parallel slit mouth area-cheek mutilations (63, 64, 65) and a related "box mouth" mutilation (e.g., Medioni and Pinto 1941: Pls. 41-42). Cf. the similar four-figure scene in the Rivera collection (México, Secretaría de Educación Pública 1946: Fig. 35). Decorated areas somewhat resemble Morett black-on-white ceramic type (Meighan, ms.).

Cf. 23.
H. 10½" W. 15"

21 Seated Girl, Nayarit. Holding pointed headdress (cf. 22) and circular fan, wearing broad loincloth, headband, earplugs, noserings, necklace, and armlets. White and black painted decoration on red-brown slip.
H. 5¾" W. 4" D. 4"

22 Boy Eating, Nayarit. Eating taco or holding tube (?), wearing pointed headdress above a kind of headcloth (cf. 21), large round earplugs, noseplug, necklace, sleeveless shirt, and loincloth. White and black painted decoration on red slip.
H. 7" W. 3½" D. 3½"

23 "Ceremonial Dance II," Nayarit. Two nude males, rod through cheeks, emaciated ridged backs. Black and red decoration on cream slip. Cf. 20.
H. 6" L. 6" D. 3"

24 Sick Woman, Nayarit. Seated, in a partially rising position, wearing headdress, necklace, earrings, nose rings, and loincloth, raised eruptions pierced with holes on face and body; black, white, and yellow designs on burnished red slip. A number of representations of this type are known. Cf. 43.
H. 10¼" W. 8½" D. 5"

21

22

23

24

25 LEFT: Drummer, Nayarit. Wearing headband, earrings, and necklace, black and white on burnished red slip. San Sebastián Red type found on both sides of the Nayarit-Jalisco border.
H. 10″ W. 3½″ D. 5½″

26 "The Jam Session," Nayarit (?). Three seated musicians on long bench (flutist, drummer, and player of tortoise shell "drum" ?). All three figures wear headbands, with a reversed bird image above that of the figure on the left and circles decorating that of the figure on the right. White and red painted decorations on buff.
H. 6½″ L. 6½″ D. 3½″

27 "Wedding Feast," Nayarit. Circular, many figures. Red on cream slip decoration.
H. 5½″ Diam. 7½″

28 Man Wearing Serape, Nayarit. A well-recognized type, usually with the tall pointed headdress, round earspools (cf. Lumholtz 1902, Vol. 2 : 302), and a height of three to four inches. White and black painted designs on the red-slipped mantle covering the body of the figure.
H. 15″ W. 9″

29 Two Striped Dogs, Nayarit. Joined, white on red slip.
H. 4½″ W. 6¼″ D. 4½″

26

27

28

29

30 LEFT: "House by Moonlight," Nayarit. White and yellow decoration on partially burnished red slip. Three joined structures, two different roof types. Note parrots and ravens on eaves, an unusual feature.
H. 12″ W. 10″ D. 8″

31 "The Wake," Nayarit. Six figures around prone body on tripod plate. Possibly a mourning scene. White and black decorations on red slip.
H. 3″ Diam. 5″

32 Joined Figures, Nayarit. Seated, forming a tripod. Headdresses are of a type common in the smaller Nayarit figures. White painted decoration on burnished red slip (with indications of necklaces and armlets).
H. 2½″ W. 2½″ D. 1¾″

33 Couple, Nayarit. Two figures on a tripod plate wear thick striped headbands (in the case of the reclining one combined with a very tall headdress), necklaces, and the more upright figure a nosering, white and black painted decorations on red slip. A shamanistic curing scene?
H. 4¾″ W. 4⅜″ D. 6½″

34 Ceremonial Ball Game, Nayarit. White on red slip. Five (originally 7 or 8?) players, nineteen (originally more) spectators (2 with conch shell trumpets [game officials?]). Apparently, the usual Mesoamerican version of the game, in which the ball could only be struck by the elbows, hips, or knees, with a player in the act of making a hip shot (size of the ball possibly exaggerated). Differs from such ball courts as the one at Chichén Itzá in that there is no ring through which the ball is passed. Missing part of the ball court would be a repeat of the other complete end of the piece. Note markers (goals? "tees"?; stone examples were found in the Amapa ball court excavated in 1959 [Clune 1963]) at the center of court. Vertical walls of ranges, with benches (architectural features, in general, display many similarities to Amapa ball court). Cf. similar—if somewhat more elaborate—example in Rivera collection (color plate in *Fondo de la Plástica Mexicana* 1964: Pl. 68).
H. 5½″ L. 13″ W. 8″

31

32

33

34

35 LEFT: Pole Ceremony, Nayarit. On tripod circular plate: ritual performer on top of pole, another figure near base, and various seated figures surrounding pole. All figures wear tall pointed headdresses. White painted decoration on red slip. Other representations of this remarkable pole ceremony are known (e.g., Bernal 1949; Von Winning and Stendahl 1969: Pl. 155). It has been identified as a version of the *volador* or "flying pole dance" of the Mesoamerican heartland (Bernal 1949; Von Winning and Stendahl 1969: 75), but is probably a distinct, though possibly related, ritual.
H. 8" Diam. 6"

36 Man with Dog under Umbrella, Nayarit. Red-orange on burnished light cream slip (traces of black), round 3-legged stool.
H. 7¼" W. 4½" D. 4"

37 Man and Child, Nayarit. Red decoration on cream slip. Style similar to the small figures of the "house groups."
H. 3½" W. 2" D. 2"

38 "House at Noonday," Nayarit. Red and black decorations on cream slip. Two joined structures with different types of peaked roofs, both with the common diamond motifs as decorative devices (see Von Winning, ms.). Note two "basements."
H. 11½" W. 8" D. 6"

36

37

38

Although these "Zacatecas" pieces are grouped
in this section for convenience, it should be
pointed out that on the basis of available
archaeological knowledge (see Bell 1969)
most of them appear to derive from a restricted
area in northeastern Jalisco centered on
Teocaltiche and perhaps adjoining Zacatecas.

39

39 "Duet," "Zacatecas" style. A seated nude male with hands on knees and drum (?) held in hands, same color scheme and techniques as 40 and 41.
H. 16½" W. 12"
Seated nude female with hands on hips, wearing large earspools, same color scheme and techniques as 42.
H. 14" W. 8"
These figures are found in burials associated with ceramic vessels often also decorated in the resist or negative painting technique (e.g., McBride 1969, Pl. 2: C, F-J). One cemetery site has recently been located near Teocaltiche, Jalisco, close to the border of Zacatecas (Delgado 1969: 49-52; Bell 1969). Two radiocarbon dates (Taylor 1970: 254) indicate a ca. A.D. 200 date for one burial in this cemetery—which suggests the general contemporaneity of this distinctive type of figure with the large hollow figures of the shaft-chamber tomb tradition farther west.

40 "Singing Man," "Zacatecas" style. Seated nude, hair tied in form of horns, arms resting on knees, black and white painted decoration on red bluff slip (including resist technique). Cf. 39, 41.
H. 16½" W. 10"

41 Drummer, "Zacatecas" styles. Seated male nude, hair tied in form of horns, arms on knees holding drum (?), same decorative color scheme and techniques as 40.
H. 15¼" W. 9½"

42 "Singer," "Zacatecas" style. Seated female nude with hands on hips, wearing large earspools, white on red slip painted decoration (some resist technique). Cf. 39 right.
H. 15" W. 7½"

40

41

42

43 Sick Man, Nayarit. Seated, legs crossed, raised
   eruptions cover face and body, black painting
   on burnished cream slip. Sick male figures are
   rarer than figures of sick women.
   H. 5½″ W. 3¾″ D. 3¼″

44 Seated Man, Nayarit. Hands on knees, partial
   red slip, on buff, wearing earrings. Example of
   a recognizable Nayarit sub-type, often featur-
   ing figures with a "hooded" effect to the apparent hairdo (e.g., Von Winning and Stendahl
   1969: Pl. 170).
   H. 26″ W. 15″ D. 13″

45 Stacked Bowls, Nayarit. A single vessel, red on
   cream slip. Cf. 46.
   H. 3¼″ D. 3½″

46 Stacked Bowls, Nayarit. A single vessel, red

43

44

on cream slip (oxide staining). Cf. 45.
H. 3″ D. 3½″

47 Incense Burners, Nayarit. With attached spoons. White slip. Probably Postclassic. These incense burners are identical to Postclassic pieces found at Amapa, Nayarit.
H. 4″ D. 2½″; H. 3″ D. 2¼″

48 Pectoral, Nayarit. Crescent shape, serrations along upper edge, red-on-buff ceramic. Pectorals of this type are frequently depicted on Nayarit figures (e.g., 14, 16, 19). Cf. 49.
L. 10″ W. 3″ D. ¾″

49 Pectoral, Nayarit. Crescent-shaped stone. Seven pairs of holes drilled along upper edge. Cf. 48.
L. 7½″ W. 2″ D. ½″

50 Trumpet, Nayarit. Conch shell with incised designs. A shaft-chamber tomb at Las Cebollas, near Tequilita, southern Nayarit, contained 125 specimens of these conch shells (many decorated with the same kinds of designs; Furst 1966). *Fasciolaria* cf. *princeps* Sowerby, 1825; occurs in the Caribbean and the Pacific.
H. 4½″ W. 5¼″ D. 10¼″

51 Raspa, Nayarit. Musical instrument, a stone rasp (*"omichicahuaztli"*). Nayarit ceramic figures are frequently shown playing this typically Mesoamerican instrument (e.g., México, Secretaría de Educación Pública 1946: Fig. 21; Von Winning and Stendahl 1969: Pl. 176).
L. 7½″ W. 2″ H. 1″

52 Atlatl Finger Loops, Nayarit (?). Stone. These U-shaped objects were attached to the wood shafts of spear-throwers, a preeminent Meso-american weapon, and are not uncommon in collections (see Ekholm 1962; Long 1966: 216). The projections on the outer curved portions may be much deteriorated zoomorphic effigies (cf. Ekholm 1962: Fig. 1 e j, k).
L. 2″

53 Three Burnishing Stones, Nayarit. Very similar specimens were found at Amapa, Nayarit, dating to the Postclassic.
H. 1″ W. 1″ L. 2″; H. 1″ W. 1″ L.1¾″; H. ¾″ W. 1½″ L. 2½″

45

46

47

48
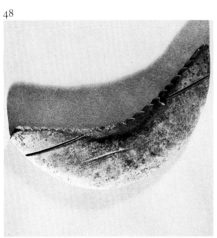

49
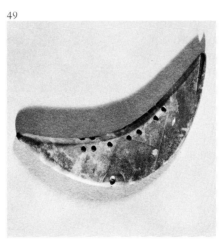

50

51

53

52

54 LEFT: "Mourner I," Nayarit. Male, knees drawn up, elbows on knees, burnished red slip. Vessel spout on neck. San Sebastián Red type found on both sides of the Nayarit-Jalisco border. Cf. 55.
H. 10½″ W. 7″ D. 8½″

55 "Mourner II," Nayarit. Seated male, knees up, arms on knees, forehead resting on arms, wearing "band headdress," earrings, and armlets; black on white decoration on burnished red slip. Vessel spout below neck. San Sebastián Red type found on both sides of the Nayarit-Jalisco border. Cf. 54.
H. 6″ W. 4″ D. 4½″

56 "Mourner III," Nayarit. Male, wearing earrings and necklace, black and white on burnished red slip. San Sebastián Red type found on both sides of the Nayarit-Jalisco border. (Published: Franz Feuchtwanger 1954, Pl. 74.)
H. 6½″ W. 6½″ D. 7½″

57 "Mourner IV," Nayarit. Seated male with knees up, left arm on knees, right elbow on left hand, right hand supports head; wearing "band headdress," earrings, necklace, and armlets; white and black on burnished red-orange slip. San Sebastián Red type found on both sides of the Nayarit-Jalisco border. Ojos Variant.
H. 14½″ W. 9″ D. 9″

58 "Mourner V," Nayarit. Seated male, one knee up, head bowed, wearing headband decorated with circular elements, earrings, and necklace, holding rattle; black on burnished red-orange slip. Vessel spout below neck. San Sebastián Red type found on both sides of the Nayarit-Jalisco border.
H. 8″ W. 7″ D. 8″

55

56

57

58

59 LEFT: Licing (?), Nayarit. Joined couple, wearing earrings and armlets, black and white painting on burnished red slip. San Sebastián Red type found on both sides of the Nayarit-Jalisco border.
H. 7″ W. 4½″ D. 3″

60 Reclining Man I, Nayarit. Nude, legs crossed, arms behind back, wearing earrings and necklace, burnished red and light cream (on face) slips, black on hair. San Sebastián Red type found on both sides of the Nayarit-Jalisco border.
H. 7″ W. 4″ D. 7¾″

61 Reclining Man II, Nayarit. Nude, wearing "band headdress," earrings, and necklace, black on burnished orange slip. San Sebastián Red type found on both sides of the Nayarit-Jalisco border.
H. 10″ W. 6″ D. 9½″

62 "Mourners," Nayarit. Male figure, upraised arm, emaciated, wearing earrings, nosering, necklace, and armlets; black and white on burnished red slip.
H. 12″ W. 5″ D. 6″
Male figure, arms crossed, emaciated, wearing earrings, nosering, and armlets; black and white on burnished red slip.
H. 12″ W. 5½″ D. 7″
Female figure, knees upraised, hands on knees, chin on hands, emaciated, wearing earrings, necklace, and armlets; black and white on burnished red slip (resist decoration on lower body). All San Sebastián Red type found on both sides of the Nayarit-Jalisco border.
H. 8¾″ W. 5½″ D. 5½″

63 "Siamese Twins," Nayarit. Joined males, wearing earrings, noserings, and necklaces; both display parallel slit mouth area-cheek mutilations (cf. 64, 65). Figure on right holds rattle. Black decorations on burnished red slip. San Sebastián Red found on both sides of the Nayarit-Jalisco border.
H. 12″ W. 9″ D. 5½″

60

61

62

63

64 Warrior and Mate (No. 65), Nayarit. Man standing, holding long mace, wearing woven bicorn helmet and body "armor," earrings, noserings, and necklace; black and white on burnished red slip, parallel slit mutilations in mouth area and on cheeks (cf. 63, 64). San Sebastián Red type found on both sides of the Nayarit-Jalisco border.
H. 27″ W. 12″ D. 9½″

65 Woman, hands on stomach, wearing earrings, noserings, necklace, and armlets; black and white on burnished red slip. Parallel slit mutilations around mouth and cheeks (cf. 63, 64), San Sebastián Red type found on both sides of the Nayarit-Jalisco border.
H. 30″ W. 13″ D. 9¼″

66 Woman with Garters, Nayarit. Seated nude, on a two-footed stool, hands on waist, wearing earrings and bands below knees, black on burnished red-brown slip (including some resist). Variant of San Sebastián Red type found on both sides of the Nayarit-Jalisco border.
H. 18″ W. 8″ D. 9″

67 Kneeling Nude, Nayarit. Woman wearing headband, earrings, and necklace; white paint on burnished red slip plus some black (resist technique). Vessel spout on head. San Sebastián Red type found on both sides of the Nayarit-Jalisco border; Ojos Variant.
H. 15″ W. 7½″ D. 7½″

68 Woman with Snake Skirt, Nayarit. Wearing headband, earplugs and skirt with S-shaped double-headed serpent designs (black on white). Black and white painted decorations on red slip. Representative of a type somewhat intermediate between San Sebastián Red and a Jalisco type characterized by elongated, narrow heads, "pointed" ears, round earplugs, and considerable white painted decoration (e.g., Marks 1968: 15, upper left). Cf. 73.
H. 17″ W. 10½″ D. 4½″

69 RIGHT: Standing Nude, Nayarit. Nude, wearing earrings and necklace (with white stripes), burnished red slip. San Sebastián Red type found on both sides of the Nayarit-Jalisco border.
H. 21″ W. 9½″ D. 8½″

64

65

66

67

68

70 Orange Dog, Nayarit. Vessel, burnished red slip with black designs (resist technique), spout on back. Cf. 71.
H. 6" L. 10" W. 6½"

71 Two Orange Dogs, Nayarit. Vessel, black spiral designs (resist technique) on burnished red slip. Cf. 70, Dockstader 1964: Pl. 6 (attributed to Jomulco, Nayarit).
H. 5¾" W. 8" L. 12¼"

72 "Four Dogs Drinking," Nayarit. Vessel, black painting on burnished bright orange slip.
H. 4" D. 5½"

73 Standing Woman, Nayarit. Virtually identical in posture and costume to 68, black and white on burnished red, incised vertical "hem" band on wrap-around skirt.
H. 27" W. 11" D. 8"

70

71

72

73

JALISCO

...rior, Jalisco. Wearing
..., earrings, noserings, and neck and
shoulder bands, holding "mace dagger" threat-
eningly and circular shield, light cream slip
with red painted decoration. Ameca Gray type.
H. 12″ W. 6½″ D. 9″

75 "The Lovers," Jalisco. Man, nude, seated cross-
legged; woman, wearing skirt, kneeling; both
wearing "crested headdress," burnished dark
red brown slip. Related to Ameca Gray type.
H. 15″ W. 16″ D. 13″

75

76 LEFT: Woman, Jalisco. Kneeling, wearing "criss-cross turban," ear pendants, and skirt; burnished cream slip with red overpaint. Excellent example of Ameca Gray type. Cf. México, Secretaría de Educación Pública 1946: Pl. 52.
H. 20″ W. 12″ D. 6″

77 Mother and Child, Jalisco. Black and red painted decorations on yellowish slip.
H. 5½″ W. 3½″ D. 2″

78 Seated Man, Jalisco. Wearing "crossed band headdress," armbands, and short trousers. Light cream slip. Ameca Gray type.
H. 18¼″ W. 12″ D. 11″

79 Seated Figure, Jalisco. Burnished dark red brown slip. Related to Ameca Gray type (with some features of the San Sebastián Red type). The hand in front of mouth gesture is unusual.
H. 12″ W. 8″ D. 7½″

80 Eunuch (?), Jalisco. Nude, seated, holding food-filled vessel, with one hand behind head, wearing earrings. Unusually realistic for Jalisco tradition. Burnished white slip with red painted decoration on lower arms and legs.
H. 11″ W. 8″ D. 8″

81 Kneeling Woman, Jalisco. Buff slip, black-painted breasts, wearing skirt. Ameca Gray type. Outstretched arm gesture is not uncommon.
H. 16″ W. 10½″ D. 8″

82 Hunchback, Jalisco. Male figure, head and arm bands, black painted decoration on burnished white slip. Ameca Gray type.
H. 12¼″ W. 10¼″ D. 8½″

77

78

79

80

81

82

83 Rite (?), Jalisco. Standing helmeted warrior
   threatening prisoner (?) with club (?), with
   traces of red paint on buff.
   H. 17″ W. 12″ D. 10″
84 RIGHT: Joined Couple, Jalisco. Man with rattle
   and fan, black and red painted decorations on
   burnished cream slip. Unusual because of color
   difference of figures. Ameca Gray type. Cf.
   Von Winning and Stendahl 1969: Pl. 135.
   H. 19½″ W. 13″ D. 11″

83

85 LEFT: "Wrestler," Jalisco. Wearing wide bossed arm and leg bands and loin cloth. Burnished cream slip with large firing clouds. Ameca Gray type.
H. 17″ W. 14″ D. 13″

86 "The King," Jalisco. Wearing tight-fitting short trousers, a protective jacket of some stiff material, a cap-like, spikey "helmet," holding a short painted rod: club (?) baton of rank (?). The largest example known. El Arenal Brown type.
H. 37″ W. 15″ D. 15″

87 Seated Woman, Jalisco. Nude, hands upraised, wearing striped headband, earrings, and arm-lets, black and red decorations on burnished cream slip. This type, with elongated, tubular head and slit eyes, has been attributed to cem-eteries in the region of San Juanito, municipio of Antonio Escobedo, about 50 miles west of Guadalajara (e.g., Parres Arias 1962).
H. 18½″ W. 12″ D. 9″

88 "Matriarch," Jalisco. Kneeling woman, black and red on white slip. Variant of San Sebastián Red type.
H. 20″ W. 10½″ D.10″

86

87

88

89 Warrior and Mate, Jalisco. Man standing, wearing bicorn helmet, earrings, necklace, armbands, and waistband, holding round striped shield and club (?), white slip with red painted designs.
H. 20″ W. 12″ D. 7″
Woman standing, white slip with red painted designs; wearing earrings, nosering, necklace, armlets, and waistband, and holding cup. Both figures represent variants of the El Arenal Brown type (with some features of both the San Sebastián Red and Ameca Gray types). Probably both were found as a pair in a single mortuary chamber or burial.
H. 20″ W. 14″ D. 7½″

90 Couple on Bench I, Jalisco. Seated on four-legged bench, woman embracing the man, cream on burnished red slip. Very similar to 91.
H. 6″ W. 4″ D. 3½″

91 Couple on Bench II, Jalisco. Seated on four-legged bench, black and cream on burnished red slip, embracing each other, both wearing turban-like headdresses; the man is nude, the woman wears a skirt. Mourning scene (?). Cf. 90.
H. 5½″ W. 5¼″ D. 3½″

92 Red Figure, Jalisco. Nude, "crest" on head, red-slipped.
H. 2¼″ W. 2″ D. 1″

93 Pectoral Nude, Jalisco. Arms on stomach, wearing necklace with pectoral and turban-like headdress, red on burnished cream slip (encrusted surface). Stylistically quite similar to 90 and 91. Cf. nearly identical piece illustrated in Vaillant 1930: Pl. XXXII, bottom row, 5 (attributed to Tala, Jalisco).
H. 7½″ W. 3″ D. 1″

94 Pregnant Woman, Jalisco. Red on cream slip. Related to San Sebastián Red type.
H. 6½″ W. 3″ D. 3″

90

91

92

93

94

95 LEFT: "Pensive Woman," Jalisco. Burnished red and buff slip, seated, wearing skirt, right knee up, right hand on knee, chin on right hand. Ameca Gray type. (Published: Rivet and Freund 1954: Pl. 29 [reversed]; Malraux 1952: Pl. 332.)
H. 14″ L. 10″ W. 9″

96 Woman Carrying a Bowl, Jalisco (?). Burnished brown-gray; stylistically somewhat aberrant, but the enormous legs relate it most closely to the San Sebastián Red type. Cf. 97, 100, 105.
H. 18″ W. 10¼″ D. 7½″

97 Performer, Jalisco (?). Nude, waistband (?), ribs (?) exaggerated, balancing ball on nose, arms form circle above head. Enormous legs connect it to Nayarit-Jalisco tradition, particularly the San Sebastián Red type. Cf. 96, 100, 105. Black slip (uneven reduction firing).
H. 16″ W. 8″ D. 5″

98 Seated Man, Jalisco. Wearing earrings, nose-ring, necklace, arm, stomach and head bands, black and white on burnished red slip. Excellent example of the El Arenal Brown type.
H. 17½″ W. 14″ D. 11″

99 "The Pot Maker," Jalisco. Seated male figure, burnished buff slip (with firing clouds), wearing "crossed bands headdress," with chin strap, and earrings, small pot at side slung from shoulder, working (?) on large pot. Ameca Gray type. (Published: Medioni and Pinto 1941: Pl. 197; México, Secretaría Pública 1946: Fig. 48.)
H. 12½″ W. 7¼″ D. 10″

100 Tripod Vessel, Jalisco (?). Anthropomorphic, female, wearing headband pierced with holes and earrings, rusty brown slip with firing clouds. Cf. 96, 97, 100.
H. 9″ D. 10″

96

97

98

99

100

101 Man on Pallet, Jalisco. Platform four-legged with low ends, white on red slip. Figure wears turban-like headdress and is covered with a large fabric (decorated with red stripes on buff). Two vertical pieces flank the head. Possibly a corpse laid out on a bier to be placed in a mortuary chamber (Delgado 1969). Cf. 102.
H. 2″ W. 4½″ D. 3⅜″

102 Man Strapped to Pallet, Jalisco. Four-legged platform, with low ends and two arched "hoops" over body. Vertical pieces flank head. Red-slipped. Cf. 101.
H. 3½″ W. 3″ L. 5″

103 "Ceramic Pillow" (?), Jalisco (?). Hollow, unslipped buff.
H. 4¼″ L. 8½″

104 Crawling Infant, Jalisco. Nude, with elongated head and headband, "nose buttons," and circular earplugs, red-slipped.
H. 4″ W. 3½″ L. 5″

105 Man with Monkey on his Back, Jalisco (?). Man's elbows on knees, man's and monkey's hands on man's head, burnished gray-brown slip. Possibly from the Guadalajara area. (cf. Parres Arias 1965b: Fig. 2). Cf. 96, 97, 100.
H. 10″ W. 7½″ D. 7″

101

104

102

105

103

COLIMA

106 Drummer, Colima. Seated man, black on burnished red slip. Wears same headdress as trumpeter.
H. 15″ W. 9½″ D. 10¾″
Trumpeter, Colima. Seated man, black on burnished red slip, wearing headdress with projecting shallow bowl-like element (shell?), holding fan (?), shell trumpet resting on left leg.
H. 15¾″ W. 15½″ D. 11¼″

107 RIGHT: Man Wearing Necklace, Colima. Seated nude, burnished dark red slip, left arm on right leg, right arm raised in "speaking pose," wearing headdress, earspools, and necklace of large leaf-shaped "scooped out" elements, probably shell sections (cf. 203).
H. 14″ W. 8½″ D. 9″

108 Drum, Colima. Vessel, burnished red slip with encrustations on drum body, little cones over "drum" surface. Spikey protuberances of this type are most frequently found on incense burners in Mesoamerica.
H. 9½" W. 7" D. 8"

109 Seated Drummer, Colima. Vessel, burnished red slip with black inclusions, wearing head-dress with projecting "tabs," drinking from bowl, spout of vessel projects from back. A good example of a recognizable Colima type, characterized particularly by hollow eye sockets (originally containing shell inlays). Cf. 116.
H. 9¾" W. 4¾" D. 8"

110 Standing Nude, Colima. Female figure, burnished buff slip (surface partially eroded).
H. 7½" W. 8¼" D. 3½"

111 Reclinatorio, Colima. Aviform vessel supported by man with tumpline, red on burnished orange slip. These backrests (cf. 147 F, L, M) are well-known in collections, but this type, supported by a figure, is very rare.
H. 10½" W. 8½" D. 11"

112 Man Carrying Pot, Colima. One knee on ground, pot carried with tumpline, red-slipped, man is orange-slipped (both burnished).
H. 15" W. 7¼" D. 12¾"

113 RIGHT: Seated Man, Colima. Vessel, burnished dark red slip with black spotted patina, knees drawn up, elbows resting on knees, chin resting on arms, wearing apparent headdress, with forehead horn, earspools, and waistband.
H. 12" W. 7" D. 10"

108

109

110

111

112

114 Phallic Dancer, Colima. Effigy vessel, burnished red slip, apparently accoutered in a kind of "armor" which includes a girdle to which is attached an exaggerated phallus. Also probably wears a mask or headpiece with a projecting "bill" and high "crest" (which also serves as the spout). Similar putative masks are known on other Colima figures (e.g., Von Winning and Stendahl 1969: Pls. 70, 83).
H. 12½″ W. 8″ D. 6½″

115 Phallic Figure, Colima. Wearing a kind of "crested helmet," red on burnished slip, seated, legs spread, leans backward, hands on ground behind him. Good example of a relatively frequent type.
H. 9½″ D. 9″ W. 7½″

116 "Priest," Colima. Vessel, buff-orange slip, standing, holding a twisted staff and rattle, wearing a distinctive headdress with a canine head, depending "earflaps," crescentic pectoral, cross-slung side pouches, and aviform penis-sheath (?). Spout issues from back. Ritual performer and/or shaman or priest? Cf. 109.
H. 10″ W. 7″ D. 7″

117 RIGHT: Seated Man, Colima. Missing right arm, left arm missing below elbow, legs flat on ground, heels touching, small "horn" on forehead, burnished red slip with numerous black inclusions. Originally the figure probably held bowl on lap.
H. 12½″ W. 10″ D. 9½″

114

116

115

118 LEFT: Seated Warrior, Colima. Vessel, figure wears short-sleeved shirt and tight-fitting short trousers, horned headdress with chin strap and oval pectoral, holding curved object (club? boomerang?), burnished red slip (with traces of white on pectoral), scattered black patina. Vessel spout issues from top of head. A fine example of a frequent Colima theme (e.g., Furst 1965 C: Fig. 4). (Published [color]: Von Winning and Stendahl 1969: Pl. 69.) H. 14″ W. 13″ D. 9″

119 Acrobat I, Colima. Vessel, orifice on stomach. Figure in backbend position, wears a kind of "skirt" and crescentic pectoral, burnished red slip with black inclusions. While "acrobat" figures are known in collections, high arched backs are rare. Cf. 121. H. 9½″ W. 8″ D. 13″

120 Cargador with Five Pots, Colima. Vessel, figure orange-slipped, pots red-slipped (some black patina). (See cover.) H. 10½″ W. 9½″ D. 10½″

121 Acrobat II, Colima. Vessel, orifice on stomach. Nude figure in back-bend position, burnished red slip with some black patina. The flatter arch is more frequently seen than the high arched back. Cf. 119. H. 9″ L. 12″ W. 10″

122 Drinker, Colima. Seated, arms upraised, holding bowl in right hand, wearing earplugs and noseplug, horned headdress with chin strap, crescentic pectoral, and off-shoulder pouch or mantle, burnished red and orange, engraved designs on headbands and pouch or mantle. (Published: Von Winning and Stendahl 1969: Pl. 75 [color].) H. 13″ W. 11¾″ D. 8¼″

119

120

121

122

123 LEFT: Head Pot, Colima. Prominent horn above forehead, nose plug, and ridges in temporal regions, vessel spout on top of head, burnished red slip (with large firing cloud). Various similar specimens are known (e.g., Furst 1965 c: Fig. 7).
H. 7″ W. 6¾″ D. 8½″

124 "The Offering," Colima. Seated man, arms outstretched, wears earplugs, "crossed bands headdress," and short-sleeved shirt (with engraved checkerboard design), burnished red slip.
H. 15″ W. 10½″ D. 10″

125 Seated Man, Colima. Nude, wearing earspools and necklace with ring pectoral, right hand missing, buff slip. A distinctive, rare Colima type (cf. Anton 1965: Pl. 55).
H. 13″ W. 8″ D. 9″

126 Seated Man, Colima. Burnished orange slip, much black patina, knees drawn up and elbows on knees, carrying pouch with tumpline (incised design).
H. 13½″ W. 8″ D. 9″

127 Four-Heads Vessel, Colima. Burnished red slip with black inclusions, hair indicated by engraving. Cf. 128.
H. 8½″ Diam. 12″

128 Nine-Faces Vessel, Colima. Faces around shoulder, burnished red slip with black inclusions. These "face pots" are relatively frequent. Cf. 127.
H. 9″ W. 12″

124

125

126

127

128

85

129 Man Holding Head Pot, Colima. Figure seated, burnished black slip, mottled with red. Actual Colima head vessels (e.g., 123) are common.
H. 4⅜″ W. 3½″ D. 3½″

130 Seated Man, Colima. Nude, on four-legged stool, wearing headstrap with small pot attached, necklace, and armbands, partial burnished red slip (on orifice rim, headstrap, forearms, and lower legs).
H. 21½″ W. 13″ D. 12″

131 Slingshot Warrior, Colima. Vessel, figure wearing "crested helmet" with "earflaps," short-sleeved shirt, and loincloth, red and white on burnished orange slip. Spout issues from back of head.
H. 12″ W. 7″ D. 5″

132 Mother and Child, Colima. Mother wearing pointed turban headdress and skirt, both wearing necklaces and armbands, white and black on unslipped buff, some black patina.
H. 11½″ W. 6½″ D. 6½″

133 Two Women, Colima. Effigy vessels, nude figures with necklaces, burnished reddish brown slip. Figure on left with earspools. Orifices of vessels at tops of heads. These distinctive figures have been attributed to the Coahuayana Valley (boundary between Colima and Michoacán; McBride 1969: Pl. 41).
H. 6½″ W. 5″ D. 2½″

134 RIGHT: Jorobado, Colima. Hunchback, burnished buff-gray slip with black patina, holes in ear lobes and for eyes. Hunchbacked figures are renowned in Colima collections, but pierced eyes are extremely rare in any Colima figure.
H. 9″ W. 8″ D. 8″

129

130

131

132

133

135 LEFT: Tall Man, Colima. Solid body, legs hollow, very flat, wearing "criss-cross turban" with asymmetric "horn," earspools, necklace, armlets, and triangular loincloth, holding mace (baton?); burnished mottled orange and black slip. Face is nearly identical to the figures of 133, so this type too may hail from the Coahuayana Valley (cf. Medioni and Pinto 1941: Pl. 41). McBride (1969: 41) believes ths type is connected with the "H4 figurine" of the Basin of Mexico Late Preclassic (Ticoman IV), a type also "associated with the Chupícuaro figuring tradition"—and thus a relatively early date (ca. 150 B.C.?) for this Colima type is a possibility.
H. 22¼" W. 10¼" D. 4½"

136 "The Quarrel," Colima. Joined couple, solid buff (traces of white paint), both wearing turban-like headdresses—man wears large ear pendants, necklace, pointed beard, and loincloth, woman wears necklace with pectoral and skirt.
H. 4½" W. 5" D. 3"

137 Acrobat, Colima. Whistle, figure in handstand position, buff, wearing turban-like headdress with chinstrap (and mask?) and "skirt." (Cf. Von Winning and Stendahl, 1969: Pl. 59).
H. 3½" W. 1¾" D. 2½"

138 Ruler (?) Carried on Litter, Colima. Litter with circular canopy conveyed by four bearers. Note unusual coiffures (headdresses?). Unslipped buff, some patina.
H. 3¾" W. 4" D. 2¾"

139 Procession, Colima. Unslipped buff.
H. 3½" W. 2" D. 3¼"

136

137

138

139

140 Pregnant Woman, Colima. Wearing short skirt, solid, unslipped reddish-buff.
H. 5″ W. 2½″ D. 1½″

141 Nude, Colima. Solid, unslipped buff-orange, wearing pointed "turban," triple necklace, and double armbands.
H. 13″ W. 6½″ D. 1½″

142 Nude Holding Dog I, Colima. Solid, wearing "turban," thick necklace, and double armbands, black painted decorations on unslipped reddish-buff. Cf. 143.
H. 1¼″ W. 5¼″ D. 2¾″

143 Nude Holding Dog II, Colima. Solid, wearing high pointed "turban," black painted decorations on unslipped reddish-buff. Cf. 142.
H. 1½″ L. 6″ W. 3″

144 Nude Woman, Colima. Solid, burnished brown-buff slip. These flattish figures with "athletic builds" constitute a distinct and readily recognizable Colima type, with the heads exhibiting a considerable range, from "realistic" to "abstract."
H. 7″ W. 4″ D. 1″

145 Joined Couple, Colima. Wearing turban-like headdresses or coiffures, double armbands, solid, unslipped reddish buff (black lines on lower bodies).
H. 4″ W. 3¼″ D. 1″

146 Reclining Nude, Colima. Solid, buff, wearing a thick headband with perforations and double armbands.
H. 3½″ L. 5″ W. 3½″

140

141

144

145

142

143

146

147 Group of Small Figures, Colima. These small figures (all whistles except I), reportedly found in the same mortuary chambers with large, hollow figures, illustrate a wide range of cultural activities, particularly ritual aspects. All are unslipped buff, some with black or white painted decorations.

A "Announcer" (figure in "speaking stance").
  H. 5″ W. 4″ D. 3½″

B Barking Dog.
  H 1¾″ W. 1¾″ D. 1¾″

C Phallic Dancer—Arm Behind Head.
  H. 4″ W. 3″ D. 3″

D Adolescent Phallic Dancer Blowing Conch.
  H. 3″ W. 1¾″ D. 1¾″

E Phallic Dancer—Arms to the Rear.
  H. 4″ W. 3″ D. 3″

F Man with Fan in Hand Leaning Against Reclinatorio (cf. 111).
  H. 3½″ W. 2½″ D. 3″

G Adolescent Warrior with Slingshot.
  H. 3½″ W. 2½″ D. 2½″

H Warrior with Slingshot.
  H. 5″ W. 3½″ D.3″

I Figure Seated on "Canopy Throne."
  H. 4″ W. 3″ D. 1½″

J Hunchback (ruler's page?).
  H. 3″ W. 2″ D. 2″

K Warrior with Staff or Long Club.
  H. 4½″ W. 4″ D. 2″

L Man Leaning Against Reclinatorio (cf. III).
  H. 3½″ W. 2½″ D. 3″

M Drummer with Reclinatorio.
  H. 4″ W. 3″ D. 4″

N Conch Player.
  H. 4″ W. 2½″ D. 2″

O Drummer.
  H. 3″ W. 3½″ D. 3″

147 A,B

147 C,D,E

147 A-O

148 LEFT: Portrait Mask I, Colima. Black (reduction firing), holes in ears and forehead. Since the eyes are not pierced, these Colima masks, which are not uncommon, were obviously not actually worn by ritual performers. They may have functioned as pectorals or have been placed over the faces of the dead (on ceramic masks in pre-Hispanic Mesoamerica in general, see Borhegyi 1955). Cf. 150.
H. 9″ W. 7½″ D. 4½″

149 Yawning Man, Colima. Effigy vessel, incisions indicating hair, brown-black (reduction firing).
H. 3¾″ W. 3⅜″ D. 3¼″

150 Portrait Mask II, Colima. Black (reduction firing), holes in ears and forehead. Cf. 148.
H. 11″ W. 9½″

151 Mace, Colima. Skeuomorph, ceramic replica of a hafted double-headed (dog) stone mace, orange slipped. Small duck head projects from base of handle. For similar stone originals, see Disselhoff 1936: Abb. 12a (Colima), Sawyer 1957: 19 (attributed to Jalisco).
L. 9½″ W. 7¼″ D. 3″

149

150

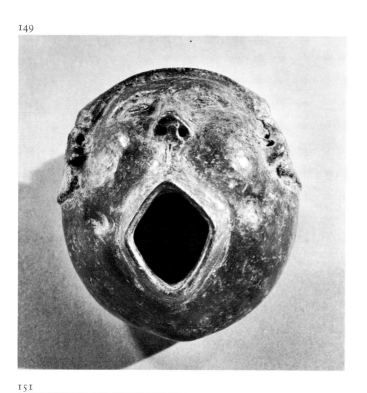

151

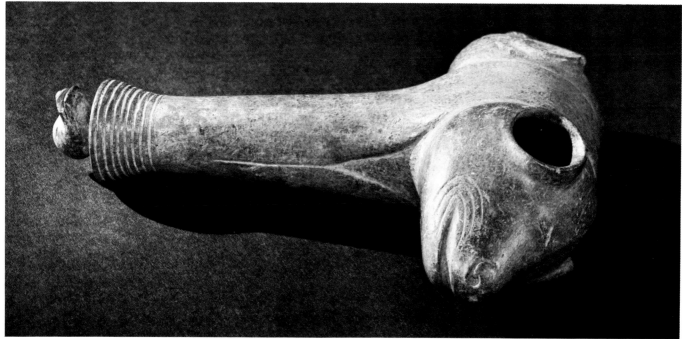

152 LEFT: Great Dog, Colima. Burnished black and red, seated, incised lines on head and upper body. An outstanding specimen of the most famous and frequent of the Colima animal figures.
H. 16½″ W. 7¾″ D. 19½″

153 Red Dog, Colima. Black showing through red, lying down, mouth open.
H. 9″ W. 7″ D. 13½″

154 Dog Wearing Mask, Colima. Vessel, human face mask, body and mask burnished buff-orange, tail and head burnished red, tail spout. Cf. well-known specimen in the Museo

Nacional de Antropolegía, Mexico, one of the first Colima tomb pieces to be published (Batres 1888: lam. XXIII, 5).
H. 8½″ L. 15½″ W. 7″

155 Coati, Colima. Vessel, nibbling on stick (stylized maize ear?), black painted decoration on burnished red slip (little gouged lines on body), spout-tail (cf. Sawyer 1957: 10-11).
H. 4½″ L. 8¼″ W. 5″

156 Curled Dog, Colima. Vessel burnished orange slip, spout issues from back.
H. 6¾″ W. 8″ D. 10″

153

154

155

156

157 Dog with Turtle Shell, Colima. Vessel, burnished orange slip with black inclusions. Spout
issues from rear of shell. Various of these com-
posite animals are known.
H. 8″ W. 6″ D. 13″

158 Sleeping Dog, Colima (?). Vessel, pouring
spout on ear, light cream slip, painted black
in parts. Probably Postclassic (Toltec horizon).
H. 6½″ W. 8½″ D. 13″

159 Lizard, Colima (?). Whistle, burnished red on
white stripes.
H. ¾″ L. 2″ W. 1″

160 Monkey (?), Colima (?). Vessel, orifice in
black, burnished orange slip with black
painted decorations (resist technique).
H. 6½″ W. 4″ D. 3½″

161 Gophers, Colima. Vessels, burnished brown-
orange slip. Spout in tail.
H. 4″ W. 4¼″ D. 9½″
Red spout on stomach.
H. 3¾″ W. 3¾″ D. 6¼″

158

159

160

161

162 Turtle, Colima. Vessel, burnished red slip (much white rootlet calcification), engraved designs on shell—from which spout issues.
H. 5″ L. 11½″ W. 9″

163 Crab, Colima. Vessel, burnished red.
H. 8″ W. 5½″ D. 7″

164 Horned Toad, Colima. Burnished orange slip mottled with black.
H. 7¼″ W. 9″ L. 15½″

165 RIGHT: Four Fish, Colima. Vessel, burnished red slip (with firing clouds).
H. 13″ D. 8½″

162

163

164

166 LEFT: Joined Frogs, Colima. Vessel, burnished
black slip with engraved designs.
H. 6″ W. 3¾″ D. 5½″

167 Mouse, Colima (?). Atop three-footed burnished gray-black "tapadera" (cover over
incense?) Postclassic?
H. 3¾″ Diam. 6½″

168 Frog, Colima (?). Vessel with orifice on animal's back, burnished cream slip with orange

and black painted decoration.
H. 3¼″ L. 5″ W. 4″

169 Iguana Vessel, Colima. Burnished red slip with
black inclusions.
H. 11″ Diam. 10″

170 Double-Headed Snake, Colima. Vessel, burnished orange (reduced to black) slip, with
engraved circles.
H. 3¾″ W. 6¼″ D. 9″

167

168

169

170

171

172

173

174

171 Water Bird, Colima. Vessel, burnished orange on buff-orange.
   H. 13½″ W. 6″ D. 5½″

172 Turkey, Colima. Whistle, spread tail feathers, unslipped buff. Cf. Disselhoff 1932: Fig. 10; Van Giffin-Duyuis 1959: Abb. 4.
   H. 2½″ W. 3½″ L. 2½″

173 Duck Head, Colima. Vessel, burnished orange slip. Bird and animal head pots are much rarer than human head pots.
   H. 4½″ W. 3½″ D. 7½″

174 Roadrunner, Colima. Ocarina, unslipped buff.
   H. 4″ L. 4¼″ W. 3¼″

175 Parrot, Colima. Vessel, burnished red slip, cream on face and beak, spout issues from back of head. (Published: Von Winning and Stendahl 1969: Pl. 97.)
   H. 10½″ L. 11″ W. 6½″

176 Duck Family, Colima. Three-duck vessel, burnished red on buff-orange slip.
   H. 8¼″ W. 10″ D. 9″

177 Owl, Colima. Vessel, burnished orange slip (reduced to black; eroded surface), incised lines on wings. Tall spout rises from back.
   H. 10¼″ W. 8¼″ D. 9″

175

177

176

178 LEFT: Cactus Vessel, Colima. Four-organo, burnished red slip with black inclusions.
H. 10″ Diam. 9½″

179 Squash Vessel I, Colima. Five squashes (?) on shoulder, burnished red slip with black inclusions.
H. 7″ W. 10½″

180 Phytomorphic Vessel, Colima. Fruit forms (?), burnished red slip with black inclusions.
H. 8¾″ D. 12¼″

181 Lobed Vessel, Colima. Four lobes or bulbs on body, burnished red slip with black decoration (resist technique).
H. 9″ W. 11″

182 Phytomorphic Vessel, Colima. Burnished red slip.
H. 8½″ Diam. 12½″

183 Vessel, Colima. Burnished red slip with black inclusions.
H. 10″ W. 8½″ D. 4″

184 Fruit Vessel, Colima. Burnished red slip with black inclusions.
H. 9″ D. 11½″

185 Doughnut-Shaped Vessel, Colima. Burnished red with black inclusions. This distinctive vessel form, here a miniature, is particularly characteristic of the Chupícuaro tradition centered in southern Guanajuato-northern Michoacán

(Peterson 1955; for its pan-Mesoamerican distribution, see Parsons 1963); cf., however, zoomorphic example attributed to Zapotiltic, Jalisco (Lumholtz 1902, Vol. II; 333).
H. 1¾″ D. 2½″

186 Cubical Vessel, Colima. Burnished red slip (eroded surface). Straight sides are unusual in Colima.
H. 7″ W. 7″ D. 7″

187 Fluted Vessel, Colima. Stylized woman's face on rim and numerous parallel flutings on upper surface of globular body of pot. Probably from Periquillo area. Postclassic?
H. 10″ C. 9″

179

180

181

182

183
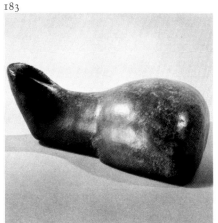

184

185

186

187

188 Vessel, Colima. Three-man tripod support, burnished red slip with black inclusions.
H. 11″ Diam. 14″

189 Parrot Pot, Colima. Three parrots support a globular, gadrooned vessel, burnished red slip with black inclusions. These vessels are frequently found in Colima tombs.
H. 9½″ D. 14″

190 Teardrop Vessel, Colima. Burnished red slip.
H. 14″ D. 9½″

191 Vessel, Colima. Burnished red (reduced to black) slip.
H. 8″ Diam. 15″

192 Jug, Colima. Handled (skeuomorphic? handle to facilitate carrying with pole?), black designs on burnished red slip (cf. Von Winning and Stendahl 1969: Pl. 107).
H. 13″ D. 7″

189

190

191

192

193

194

195

196

197

193 Squash Vessel II, Colima. Burnished gray-
brown slip (reduction firing).
H. 7″ L. 10″ W. 6″

194 Tied Form, Colima. Vessel, burnished orange
slip (with traces of black paint).
H. 4″ W. 5½″ D. 7″

195 Five-spout Vessel, Colima (?). Burnished
gray-brown slip.
H. 4½″ C. 9″

196 Cherimoya Vessel, Colima. Burnished red slip
(cf. México, Secretaría de Educación Pública
1946: Pl. 106b).
H. 5″ D. 7″

197 Five-Sided Vessel, Colima. Burnished red slip
with black inclusions.
H. 10″ W. 9″

198 Axe Vessel, Colima. Burnished light orange slip
(with firing clouds). Probably a skeuomorphic
representation of a genuine stone "monolithic
axe." Cf. México, Secretaría de Educación Pública 1946: Pl. 105.
H. 12″ W. 10″

199 Incense Burner, Colima. Two grotesque figures,
back to back, painted black decoration (resist
technique) on unburnished orange slip (with
firing clouds), a particularly large example.

These rather grotesque pieces, frequent in collections, appear to date to the Postclassic period
and are stylistically quite distinct from the rest
of the Colima tradition.
H. 33″ W. 12″ D. 8¼″

200 Temple Model, Colima (?). Buff-orange slip
(roof lightly burnished), sacrificial stone in
front of door? Probably Postclassic.
H. 9″ L. 4½″ W. 3″

198

199

200

201 Anthropomorphic Rattle, Colima. Female form, unslipped buff.
H. 3″ W. 2″

202 Temple Models, Colima (Nayarit?). White with red roofs; sacrificial stones in front of door (?). Probably Postclassic.
H. 3¾″ W. 1¾″ D. 2″; H. 2¾″ W. 1½″

203 Necklace, Colima. (Shell), 10 pieces, shiny on underside. Necklaces of this type are probably depicted on ceramic figures (e.g., 107).

204 Incense Burner, Colima. Spikes (or hobnails) on surface, buff (encrustation on outer surface). Probably Postclassic.
H. 12¼″ D. 10″

205 Two Musicians, Colima. Shell, male figures. Playing an aerophone (panpipe?); also holds an indeterminate object in the left hand.
H. 1¾″ W. 1″
Playing an aerophone (double flute?).
H. 3″ W. 1″ D. ½″

206 Seated Man, Colima. Blue-gray jade pendant, highly polished, hole at top of head. These extremely rare small stone effigies are reported to be found occasionally in the tombs along with the ceramic pieces. Cf. Alsberg 1969: Pls. 55-59.
H. 2¼″ W. 1¾″ D. ½″

201

202

203

204

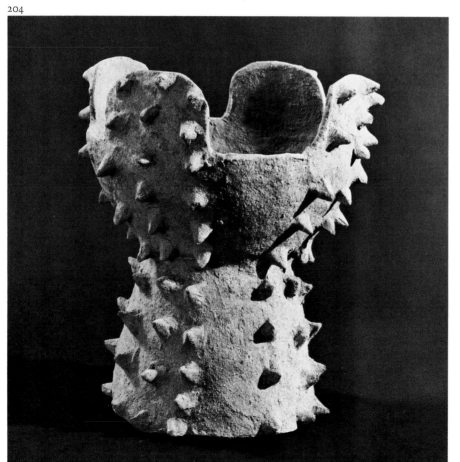

205

206

BIBLIOGRAPHY

ALSBERG, JOHN
1968 *Ancient Sculpture from Western Mexico: The Evolution of Artistic Form.* Text: John L. Alsberg, Photography: Rodolfo Petschek, Berkeley

ANONYMOUS
1960 "Fichas del catálogo del Museo de Arqueología del Occidente de México," *Eco,* 4: n.p.
1961 "Piezas arqueológicas de San Juanito, Municipio de Antonio Escobedo, Jal.," *Eco,* 6: n.p.
1962 "Fichas del catálogo del Museo de Arqueología del Occidente de México," *Eco,* 9: n.p.
1965 "Grand Rounds a Thousand Years before Columbus," *Pfizer Spectrum, 13,* 2: 26-29 (Weisman collection)
1966 "Museo de Arqueología del Occidente de México: la pieza del més," *Eco,* 25: n.p.

ANTON, FERDINAND
1965 *Alt-Mexiko und seine Kunst,* Leipzig

BASLER, ADOLPHE AND ERNEST BRUMMER
1928 *L'art précolombien,* Paris

BATRES, LEOPOLDO
1888 *Civilización de algunas diferentes tribus que habitaron el territorio hoy mexicano, en la antigüedad,* Mexico

BELL, BETTY
Report on excavations at El Cerro Encantado, ms.

BERGER, RAINER AND WILLARD LIBBY
1966 "UCLA Radiocarbon Dates V," *Radiocarbon,* 8: 467-497

BERNAL, IGNACIO
1948-1949 "Exploraciones en Coixtlahuaca, Oaxaca," *Revista Mexicana de Estudios Antropológicos,* 10: 5-76
1949 "El volador en Nayarit," *Tlalocan, 3,* 1: 92-93

BORHEGYI, STEPHAN
1955 "Pottery Mask Tradition in Mesoamerica," *Southwestern Journal of Anthropology,* 11: 205-213
1964 "Frozen in Clay," *Lore,* XIV, 3: 80-87

BRETON, ADELA
1903 "Some Mexican Portrait Figures," *Man,* 3: 130-133

BUSHNELL, G. H. S.
1965 *Ancient Art of the Americas,* London

CLUNE, FRANCIS
1963 A Functional and Historical Analysis of the Ballgame of Mesoamerica, Ph.D. dissertation, UCLA

COLLIER, DONALD
1959 "Ancient Art of Western Mexico," *Chicago Natural History Museum Bulletin, 30,* 2: 4-5

CORONA NUNEZ, JOSE
1954 "Diferentes tipos de tumbas prehispánicas en Nayarit," *Yan,* 3: 46-50
1955 *Tumba de El Arenal, Etzatlán, Jalisco,* México, Instituto Nacional de Antropología e Historia, Dirección de Monumentos Pre-Hispánicos, Informes, 3
1960 *Arqueología: Occidente de México,* Jalisco en el arte, Guadalajara

COSSIO, JOSE
1939 "Idolos de Colima," *Boletín de la Sociedad Mexicana de Geografía y Estadística,* 51: 119-205
1940 *Idolos de Colima,* Mexico

COVARRUBIAS, MIGUEL
1957 *Indian Art of Mexico and Central America,* New York

DELGADO, DIEGO
1969 Arquitectura funeraria precolombina en el estado de Jalisco, M.A. thesis, UCLA

DISSELHOFF, HANS
1932 "Note sur le résultat de quelques fouilles archéologiques faites à Colima (Mexique)," *Revista del Instituto de Etnología de la Universidad Nacional de Tucumán,* 2: 525-537
1936 "Trachtstücke und Geräte der Bewohner des alten Colima," *Baessler-Archiv,* 19: 16-21
1960 "Notizen zur Archäologie Westmexikos," *Ethnologica,* 2: 542-547

DOCKSTADER, FREDERICK
1964 *Indian Art in Middle America: Pre-Columbian and Contemporary Arts and Crafts of Mexico, Central American and the Caribbean,* New York

EKHOLM, GORDON
1956 "Art in Archaeology," *Aspects of Primitive Art,* Museum of Primitive Art, New York
1962 "U-Shaped 'Ornaments' Identified as Finger-Loops from Atlatls," *American Antiquity,* 28, 2: 181-185, Salt Lake City

FONDO DE LA PLASTICA MEXICANA
1964 *Flor y canto del arte prehispánico de México,* Mexico

FEUCHTWANGER, FRANZ
1954 *The Art of Ancient Mexico,* Photoggraphy: Irmgard Groth-Kimball, New York

FURST, PETER
1965a "Radiocarbon Dates from a Tomb in Mexico," *Science,* 147, 3658: 612-613
1965b "Datación de una tumba de tiro de Etzatlán, Jalisco," *Eco,* 22: n.p.
1965c "West Mexican Tomb Sculpture as Evidence for Shamanism in Prehispanic Mesoamerica," *Antropologica,* 15: 29-30
1965d "West Mexico, the Caribbean and Northern South America: Some Problems in New World Interrelationships," *Antropologica,* 14: 1-37
1966 Shaft-tombs, Shell Trumpets and Shamanism: a Culture-historical Approach to Problems in West Mexican Archaeology, Ph.D. dissertation, UCLA
1967 "Tumbas de tiro y cámara: un posible eslabón entre México y los Andes," *Eco,* 26: n.p.

GALINDO, MIGUEL
1922 "Bosquejo de la geografía arqueológica del Estado de Colima," *México, Anales del Museo Nacional de Arqueología, Historia y*

Etnografía, Cuarta Epoca 1: 165-178.
1923-1924 *Apuntes para la historia de Colima,* 2 vols, Colima
1925 *Geografía arqueológica del estado de Colima,* Colima

GIFFORD, EDWARD
1950 "Surface Archaeology of Ixtlán de Río, Nayarit," *University of California Publications in American Archaeology and Ethnology,* 43, 2

INSTITUTO JALISCIENSE
DE ANTROPOLOGIA E HISTORIA
1964 *Joyas del Museo de Arqueología del Occidente de México,* Introduction by Fernando González Gortazar, Guadalajara

KELLY, ISABEL
1944 "West Mexico and the Hohokam," *El norte de México y el sur de Estados Unidos* (Tercera Reunión de Mesa Redonda sobre Problemas Antropológicos de México y Centro América..., 1943): 206-222. México, Sociedad Mexicana de Antropología
1945 "The Archaeology of the Autlán-Tuxcacuesco Area of Jalisco, I: The Autlán Zone," *Ibero-Americana,* 26
1947a "An Archaeological Reconnaissance of the West Coast: Nayarit to Michoacan," *Vigesimoséptimo Congreso Internacional de Americanistas: Actas de la Primera Sesión, Celebrada en la Ciudad de México en 1939,* II: 74-77
1947b "Excavations at Apatzingan, Michoacán," *Viking Fund Publications in Anthropology,* 7, 1948 "Ceramic Provinces of Northwest Mexico," *El occidente de México* (Sociedad Mexicana de Antropología, Cuarta Reunión de Mesa Redonda sobre Problemas Antropológicos de México y Centro América): 55-71
1949 "The Archaeology of the Autlán-Tuxcacuesco Area of Jalisco, II: The Tuxcacuesco-Zapotitlán Zone," *Ibero-Americana,* 27

KIRCHHOFF, PAUL
1946 "La cultura del occidente de México a través de su arte," *México, Secretaría de Educación Pública,* 1946: 49-69

KUBLER, GEORGE
1962 *The Art and Architecture of Ancient America: The Mexican, Maya and Andean Peoples,* Baltimore

KUNIKE, HUGO
1912 "Musikinstrumente aus dem alten Michoacan," *Baessler-Archiv,* 2: 282-284

LEHMANN, HENRI
1941 "Le personnage couché sur le dos; sujet commun dans l'archéologie du Mexique et de l'Equateur," *The Civilizations of Ancient America* (Proceedings of the 29th International Congress of Americanists, New York, 1949, Sol Tax, ed.): 291-298
1953 "On Noel Morss' 'Cradled Infant Figurines,'" *American Antiquity,* 19, 1: 78-80
1964 "Maisons de Céramique (Nayarit, Mexique)" *Objets et Mondes* (la Revue du Musée de l'Homme), Paris, Vol. 4, No. 2: 107-118

LONG, STANLEY
1966 Archaeology of the Municipio of Etzatlán, Jalisco, Ph.D. dissertation, UCLA
1967 "Formas y distribución de tumbas de pozo con cámara lateral," *Razón y Fábula,* 1: 1-15

LONG, STANLEY AND R. ERVIN TAYLOR
1966a "Chronology of a West Mexican Shaft-Tomb," *Nature,* 212, 5062: 651-652
1966b "Suggested Revision for West Mexican Archeological Sequences," *Science,* 154, 3755: 1456-1459

LONG, STANLEY AND MARCIA V. V. WIRE
1966 "Excavations at Barra de Navidad, Jalisco," *Antropologica,* 18

LUMHOLTZ, CARL
1902 *Unknown Mexico,* 2 vols, New York

MALRAUX, ANDRE
1952 *Le Musée Imaginaire de la Sculpture Mondiale,* La Galerie de la Pléiade, Paris

MARKS, SHELDON
1968 *The Jules Berman Kahlúa Collection of Pre-Columbian Art,* Los Angeles

MC BRIDE, HAROLD
1969 "The Extent of the Chupícuaro Tradition," *The Natalie Wood Collection of Pre-Columbian Ceramics from Chupícuaro, Guanajuato, Mexico, at UCLA* (Jay Frierman, ed.), Occasional Papers of the Museum and Laboratories of Ethnic Arts and Technology, University of California, Los Angeles, 1: 33-49

MCBRIDE, HAROLD AND DIEGO DELGADO
Cerámica de estilo Teotihuacano en Colima, ms.

MEDIONI, GILBERT
1952 *L'art Tarasque du Mexique occidental,* Paris

MEDIONI, GILBERT AND M. T. PINTO
1941 *Art in Ancient Mexico, Collection. of Diego Rivera,* New York

MEIGHAN, CLEMENT
1961 Interrelationships of New World Cultures—Investigation by the Institute for Andean Research, supported by the National Science Foundation, field activities of Project A (West Mexico), 1960-1961, mimeographed
1962 "Cultural Similarities between Western Mexico and Andean Regions," *Mesoamerican Studies,* Research Records of the University Museum, Southern Illinois University, 4: 11-25 Archaeology of the Morett Site, Colima, ms.

MESSMACHER, MIGUEL
1966 *Colima,* Mexico, Instituto Nacional de Antropología e Historia, Colección de Libros de Arte, 1

MEXICO, SECRETARIA
DE EDUCACION PUBLICA
1946 *Arte precolombino del occidente de México,* México

MORSS, NOEL
1952 "Cradled Infant Figurines from Tennessee and Mexico," *American Antiquity,* 18, 2: 164-166

NICHOLSON, H. B.
1962 "Notes and News: Middle America," *American Antiquity,* 27, 4: 617-624
1963 "Interrelationships of New World Cultures: A Coordinated Research Program of the Institute of Andean Research, Project A: Central Pacific Coast of Mexico (Principal Investigators: Clement Meighan and H. B. Nicholson), preliminary report: third field season, 1961-1962," *Katunob,* 4: 39-51
The Cultures and Languages of the Native Peoples of Trans-Tarascan Michoacán West Mexico, ms.

NICHOLSON, H. B. AND JACK SMITH
1962 "Interrelationships of New World Cultures, Project A: Central and South Pacific Coast, Mexico. Preliminary Report, 1960 season," *Katunob,* 3: 5-8

NOGUERA, EDUARDO
1942 "Exploraciones en 'El Opeño', Michoacán," *Vigesimoséptimo Congreso Internacional de Americanistas: Actas de la Primera Sesión, Celebrada en la Ciudad de México en 1939,* I: 574-586
1955 "Apéndice: distribución de tumbas de tiro o pozo," In Corona Nuñez, 1955: 27-29
1965 *La cerámica arqueológica de Mesoamérica,* Universidad Nacional Autónoma de México, Instituto de Investigacions Históricas, primera serie, num. 86

PARRES ARIAS, JOSE
1962 "Nuevas adquisiciones del Museo de Arqueología," *Eco,* 12: n.p.
1963a "Cofradía: nueva zona arqueológica en Jalisco," *Eco,* 14: n.p.
1963b "Nuevas piezas de cerámica adquiridas por el Instituto Jalisciense de Antropología e Historia," *Eco,* 16: n.p.
1965a "Dos nuevas adquisiciones para el Museo de Arqueología del Occidente de México," *Eco,* 20: n.p.
1965b "Nuevas joyas del Museo de Arqueología del Occidente de México," *Eco,* 21: n.p.
1968 "Joya prehispánica del Museo de Arqueología del Occidente de México," *Eco,* 28: n.p.

PARSONS, LEE A.
1963 "A Doughnut-Shaped Vessel from Kaminaljuyú, with a Distributional Analysis of this Unusual Form," *American Antiquity,* 28, 3: 386-389

PETERSON, FREDERICK
1955 "'Doughnut-shaped' vessels and bird bowls of Chupícuaro, Mexico," *Ethnos,* 20, 2-3: 137-145

PINA CHAN, ROMAN
1959 *Guía de la Sala de las Culturas de Occidente,* México, Instituto Nacional de Antropología e Historia, Museo Nacional de Antropología

PORTER, MURIEL
1956 "Excavations at Chupícuaro, Guanajuato, Mexico," *Transactions of the American Philosophical Society,* New Series, 46, Part 5
1969 "A Reappraisal of Chupícuaro," *The Natalie Wood Collection of Pre-Columbian Ceramics from Chupícuaro, Guanajuato, Mexico, at UCLA* (Jay Frierman, ed.), Occasional Papers of the Museum and Laboratories of Ethnic Arts and Technology, University of California, Los Angeles, 1: 5-15

RAMIREZ FLORES, JOSE
1935 "La arqueología en el sur de Jalisco," *Boletín de la Sociedad Mexicana de Geografía y Estadistica, Junta Auxiliar Jalisciense*, 4, 2: 41-56

RAMOS MEZA, ERNESTO
1960 *Arqueopatología*, Instituto Jalisciense de Antropología e Historia, Serie Científica, 1

REDFIELD, ROBERT
1953 *The Primitive World and its Transformations*, Ithaca

RIVET, PAUL
1954 *Mexique Précolombien*, Texte de P.R., Photographies de Gisele Freund, Collection des Ides Photographiques, Paris, 8

RUBIN DE LA BORBOLLA, DANIEL
1946 "Los Tarascos," *México, Secretaría de Educación Pública*, 1946: 35-48

SAUER, CARL
1948 "Colima of New Spain," *Ibero-Americana*, 29

SAUER, CARL AND DONALD BRAND
1932 "Aztatlán: Prehistoric Mexican Frontier on the Pacific Coast," *Ibero-Americana*, 1

SAWYER, ALAN
1957 *Animal Sculpture in Pre-Columbian Art*, The Art Institute of Chicago

SCHONDUBE, OTTO
1968 *Figurillas del occidente de México*, México, Instituto Nacional de Antropología e Historia, Museo Nacional de Antropología, Colección Breve, 8
1969 "Culturas del occidente de México" (versions also in English, French, and German), *Artes de México*, No. 119, Año XVI: 5-13

TAYLOR, R. ERVIN
1970 Chronological Problems in West Mexican Archaeology: A study in the application of a dating systems approach in archaeological research. Ph.D. dissertation, UCLA
"The Shaft Tombs of Western Mexico: problems in the interpretation of religious function in non-historic archaeological contexts" (in press, *American Antiquity*), ms.

TAYLOR, R. ERVIN, RAINER BERGER, CLEMENT MEIGHAN, AND H. B. NICHOLSON
1969 "West Mexican Radiocarbon Dates of Archaeological Significance," *The Natalie Wood Collection of Pre-Columbian Ceramics from Chupícuaro, Guanajuato, Mexico, at UCLA* (Jay Frierman, ed.), Occasional Papers of the Museum and Laboratories of Ethnic Arts and Technology, University of California, Los Angeles, 1: 19-30

TOSCANO, SALVADOR
1946 "El arte y la historia del occidente en México," *México, Secretaría de Educación Pública*, 1946: 9-33

VAILLANT, GEORGE
1930 "Excavations at Zacatenco," *Anthropological Papers of the American Museum of Natural History*, 32, Part I

VAN GIFFEN-DUYVIS, GUDA
1959 "Einige Musikinstrumente aus dem Staat Colima," *Mitteilungen aus dem Museum für Völkerkunde in Hamburg*, 25: 48-52

VON WINNING, HASSO
1958 "An Unusual Incense-Burner from Colima, Mexico," *The Masterkey*, 32, 2: 40-42
1959 "Eine keramische Dorfgruppe aus dem alten Nayarit im westlichen Mexiko," *Mitteilungen aus dem Museum für Völkerkunde in Hamburg* 25: 138-143
Ceramic house models and figurine groups from Nayarit (m.s. in press, *Akten des 38. Internationalen Amerikanistenkongresses, Stuttgart-Munchen, 1968*).

VON WINNING, HASSO AND ALFRED STENDAHL
1969 *Pre-Columbian Art of Mexico and Central America*, New York

SELECTED GLOSSARY

AMECA GREY TYPE
SAN SEBASTIAN RED TYPE
EL ARENAL BROWN TYPE Names of pottery and ceramic sculpture types characteristic of West Mexico. See text references pages 62, 54, 69, for detailed descriptions

ANTHROPOMORPHIC Formed in the shape of a human figure

ATLATL A device used for propelling a spear

AVIFORM In the shape of a bird

BURNISH Surface polishing of ceramic objects usually done with a stone

"CHINESCO" A West Mexican sculpture style named by the Mexican tomb looters to signify a resemblance to oriental appearance

CONTACT The time when Europeans first reached a given Mesoamerican area and were in a position to observe and describe the native way of life. In the case of the tomb arc of West Mexico, 1522-1525.

ETHNOGRAPHIC Pertaining to customs and traditions of living or recent native peoples

MASA Ground corn meal

MESOAMERICA That region of Mexico and Central America in which the higher aboriginal civilizations of North America developed; roughly from Northern Mexico to El Salvador

METATE A stone with concave upper surface used for grinding grain

MORTUARY COMPLEX The assemblage of features found in the death rituals of a people: specifically, the tombs, burial practices, and associated grave offerings

NEGATIVE PAINTING A design on an object left in the base color by application of a coating which permits the rest of the object to be smudged or fired a darker color

PECTORAL An ornament for the breast

PHYTOMORPHIC Formed in the shape of a plant

PRE-COLUMBIAN
PRE-CORTESIAN
PRE-HISPANIC The time in Middle and South American history which predates the explorations of Columbus, the conquests of Cortes, and of the Spaniards

PROTON-MAGNETOMETER
SEISMIC HAMMER Devices for locating buried objects such as tombs

PROVENIENCE The location in which an object is found

RADIOCARBON DATING A technique for determining the age of organic specimens by the decay of carbon—14 which they contain

RESIST A technique of decoration in which part of the design is covered with a material that resists applied color

SKEUOMORPH A copy of an object ordinarily made of a different material (e.g., a pottery copy of a basket or a gourd)

SLIP A thin coating of wet clay applied to ceramic objects either before or after firing

TAPADERA A hemispheric, lid-like clay object with three or four supports placed over burning incense

TEPETATE Solidified volcanic tuff

TUMPLINE A kind of sling (with strap worn over forehead) used to carry a pack on the back

TYPOLOGY Analysis or classification based on types

ZOOMORPHIC Formed in the shape of an animal

Designed in Los Angeles by Ed Kysar,
29,000 copies were lithographed by Anderson
Lithograph Co. Typography is Garamond
with Old Style numerals. Photographs are by
Edward Cornachio and John Gebhart.